Heart to Heart

Devotional Thoughts for Women

Heather Pryor

Pryor Convictions Media
St. Petersburg, FL

Copyright © 2012 by Paul & Heather Pryor
All rights reserved.

Note to churches: If you would like permission to reprint some of these articles in your weekly bulletin, please contact the author.

Pryor Convictions Media exists to provide faith-building materials to homeschools, families and churches. For more information about our other products and publications please visit our website:

www.pryorconvictions.com

paulpryor@pryorconvictions.com

NKJV: *Scripture taken from the New King James Version®. Copyright © 1982 by Thomas Nelson, Inc. Used by permission. All rights reserved.*

Cover image photo credit:
Copyright © vaclavhroch/Shotshop.com

Table of Contents

Introduction..5

Christian Living
How Will You Be Remembered?...9
Success..11
Learning A Lesson From Robinson Crusoe..............................12
Are You Interested?...15
A Tale Of Two Influences..17
Oh Be Careful Little Mouth What You Say...............................20
Be Glad..23
Seeing Red...26
Hannah, An Example Of The Power Of Prayer.......................28
A Contented Life...31
Speaking Without Words...34
Think On These Things..36
Code Adam..38
Learning (and Loving) To Teach..41
Is Your Diffuser Working?...44
The First Five Minutes 47
Bored By The Bible?...49

Christian Womanhood & Family
Could God Have Chosen You?...55
Having A Mary Heart In A Martha World...............................58
Take Time To Be Holy..60
Gifts Of Motherhood..61
Are You A Titus 2 Woman?..64
What Gifts Will You Give Your Children?...............................67
What Will YOU Do?..71
What Is God's Purpose For Your Life?....................................74
Practical Application..78
The Proverbs 31 Woman..80
The Role Of Women...81
A Servant Of The Lord...84
God's Family...86
A Servant Of The Church, Helper Of Many............................89
The Christian Woman's Survival Kit.......................................92

Encouragement
Yes, I Can..95
Be Still And Know That I Am God..98
Waiting..101
A Lesson In Persistence...104
Be A Barnabas..106
Spring Cleaning..108
Blessings In The Midst Of Suffering......................................111

Time..114
Overcoming Discouragement: God's 3-step Process....................118
Trust In The Lord..120
Is Your Hut Burning?..122
What Are You Anchored To?...123
The Three "P's" Of Promise...126

Just For Fun
Can You Figure This Out?...131
Can You Find 20 Books Of The Bible In This Paragraph?...........132
Mystery Math..133
Rhyme Time..134
Can You Find The Common Link Between Each Set Of Items?...135
Answer Key...137
About The Author..141

Introduction

This is a book that has been years in the making – literally! In 1999, we moved to St. Petersburg, Florida, where my husband became the pulpit minister for the Northside Church of Christ. A few months after we settled, I began a monthly bulletin for the ladies of the congregation called, "Heart to Heart". The bulletins were filled with devotional articles, as well as quizzes or puzzles, poems, Bible verses, and recipes. This book is a compilation of several of the articles with a few of my favorite puzzles thrown in for fun.

My purpose in writing these articles has always been to encourage women to have a stronger, closer relationship with the Lord. Many of these articles are based on my own experiences, faults, and struggles which I hope will make them relatable to you as well. Any resemblance to anyone else may be on purpose, but is probably just coincidental.

May God bless you in your endeavors to live for Him!

~Heather Pryor

Christian Living

How Will You Be Remembered?

On February 10, 2000, my husband and his family and I, stood around the hospital bed of my father-in-law and watched him pass from this life to go on to his reward. The family had a double visitation on Saturday, the 12th and a memorial service on Sunday the 13th. The visitation yielded droves of people with lines that went on and on. The Sunday memorial service filled all of the pews in the church. It was very touching to see not only the sheer number that came out of respect and love, but the diversity of people. Along with being a gospel preacher for fifty years, my father-in law and his wife ran a printing business from their home. Several printing customers came to pay their respects to the family. Waitresses from a local restaurant where he ate often came as well. Members of churches that he had preached for thirty and forty years ago came as well as family, friends, people from the community, etc. Interestingly, those people from so many different walks of Dad's life said some of the very same things about him. They spoke of his kindness, goodness, and gentleness. They talked of his integrity and manner of life. They remembered him being a man of few words because he chose his words carefully and put thought into what he said. He was remembered for being a wonderful husband and father and above all, a faithful servant to the Lord. He did not gain this reputation among people in the last few months or weeks of his life. It was how he lived his whole life and it is what he will always be remembered for.

Matthew 26:6-13 records the incident of the woman who anointed Jesus with the expensive perfume in the alabaster box. She was being condemned for this by the disciples when Jesus says in verse 10, "*Why do you trouble this woman? For she has done a good work for me.*" He continues in verse 13, "*...what this woman has done will also be told as a memorial to her.*" Jesus wrote this woman's epitaph! Her name was not given in Scripture, but she is still remembered for doing a good work for the Lord.

Could the same be said of us if when we die? What would you be remembered for? Would it be for your outstanding community service? Your financial success? Your career? Quietly helping others behind the scenes? Or on the flip side, would you be remembered as someone who had a bad attitude? Carried a grudge? Was unkind or arrogant? Or maybe apathetic?

Oh that we should each live our lives in such a way that Jesus Himself could say at our funeral, "She has done a good work for *Me*."

****

Success

To look back at yesterday and yet
Have peace of mind and not regret.
To remember with pride and nary a frown
That you spent your time building and not tearing down.

To have won the sweet taste of victory
And know 'twas gained with integrity.
Or suffered the despair of bitter defeat
And not stooped to lying or deceit.

To know that your principles withstood every test
Ah, therein lies the real meaning of Success.
To have kept values high while accepting the scars
Truly that is reaching the unreachable stars.

~Mary Margaret Klump

This poem was written by my grandmother as a tribute to her late husband.

Learning A Lesson From Robinson Crusoe

A few weeks ago, two of my children read the book *Robinson Crusoe* in our homeschool and then I discussed it with each of them before they wrote their book reports. I had heard about the book, but had never read it for myself. In order for me to discuss it with my children and ask them pertinent questions, I needed to read the book on my own. I must say that it was very interesting and it brought some important lessons to my attention that I would like to share with you.

For those of you who may not have read this story, it is about an Englishman named Robinson Crusoe who winds up shipwrecked on a deserted island. At the time, he has no way of knowing that this island will be his home for the next twenty-eight years.

Now put yourself in his situation: You are alone on an uninhabited island and have no way to communicate with anyone. You have no shelter. You have no idea what wild animals may inhabit the island. You do not know what foods are safe and available to you. You have no way of knowing when or if you will be rescued. How would you feel? What might be the first thing that you would do? Would being thankful to God cross your mind at this time?

When Robinson was shipwrecked, the ship had wedged on a sandbar a little ways out from shore. He was able to swim out to the ship, use some of its lumber to build a raft, and salvage many things to use for his survival. As he started to explore the island, he found some wild goats which he later put into a corral that he built for them. He later had quite a large herd which provided him with plenty of milk and meat. He found sea turtles and birds for food. He found vines of wild grapes which he ate and also dried into raisins. He...well, read the book for yourselves and just see all of the things he was able to do on that island! I will tell you one more thing that he did which I found interesting. Shortly after his shipwreck, he sat down one day to take stock of his situation. He had obtained some paper and ink from the ship and he began to use it by making a list that was divided into two columns. One column listed all of the evil or bad that he could see in his situation. The other column listed all of the good he could see in his situation. For example, on the evil side he listed, "I have no clothes to speak of other than what I now wear along with a few shirts brought from the ship." Then on the good side he listed, "I am in a place with weather that is quite hot and therefore have no need of much in the way of clothes." On the evil side he would list, "I am on a deserted island with no way to obtain supplies of any kind." On the good side would read, "I was fortunate to secure many items from the ship which will be useful to my existence here." He went on to list many things that he saw as the "down side" of his shipwreck, but the interesting thing to me was that for every bad thing in his circumstances, he could see a good thing. He said, "I thought about these things, and thought about them, until it occurred to me that in even the most miserable conditions there is comfort; in despair there is yet hope. For every evil there is a better good."

The most important thing that he salvaged from the wrecked ship was a Bible. The first words he read from it were, *"Call on me in the day of trouble, I will deliver you, and you shall glorify Me."* (Psalms 50:15) After reading these words, Robinson Crusoe thanked the Lord for the blessing of deliverance from death in the sea and for blessing him so bountifully. In the midst of what seemed to be a great trial and period of suffering, Robinson was thankful to the Lord.

Are you still thinking about what you would be doing if you were in his situation? When I read this book, I thought about it and realized that making a list like that and finding ways to be thankful would probably not be what I would be doing. I would be too busy pushing the panic button!

Even though this story is fiction, we can read the words of one who truly did suffer affliction, and yet was thankful. II Cor. 11:25-27 tells us, *"Three times I was beaten with rods; once I was stoned; three times I was shipwrecked; a night and a day I have been in the deep; in journeys often, in perils of my own countrymen, in perils of the Gentiles, in perils of the sea, in perils among false brethren; in weariness and toil, in sleeplessness often, in hunger and thirst, in fastings often, in cold and nakedness..."* Yet the apostle Paul, who penned these words, was still able to say, *"Not that I speak in regard to need, for I have learned in whatever state I am, to be content."* (Philippians 4:11) Paul was also able to say, *"Rejoice always, pray without ceasing,* **in everything give thanks**; *for this is the will of God in Christ Jesus for you."* (I Thessalonians 5:16-18)

We live in the greatest country on earth with plenty of food to eat, roofs over our heads, clothes on our backs and Bibles in our hands. Let us truly be thankful for what God has so bountifully blessed us with.

****

Are You Interested?

Ask any kid you meet to talk about a subject that they are knowledgeable in and what is the response likely to be? Well, one may tell you all about a certain time period in history. Another may tell you everything you ever wanted to know about astronomy. Others may tell you all about baseball or some other sport. And, likely as not, many would tell you everything about the latest T.V. shows, movies, and video games. What would be the determining factor in what their answers would be? They will be knowledgeable about (and eager to share) what they are most interested in. Children never have to be prodded to learn something in a subject area that they personally enjoy and have a great interest in and the same is true with us as adults.

Hosea 4:6 says, *"My people are destroyed for lack of knowledge."* How's *your* Bible knowledge? Do you know the books of the Bible? Do you know the plan of salvation and some scriptures to accompany each step? How many scriptures have you memorized? The longer we're a Christian, the greater our Bible knowledge ought to be. We should be growing in the Word and learning new things from it every day. If we're not very knowledgeable in the Word of God, then that is an indication that we're not spending enough time reading and studying it. Sadly, the reason we're not doing so may be that we just don't have a whole lot of interest in it. We're like the child who has to go to school, but just doesn't want to do his homework because it's too boring. It's great to attend church and Bible class and that is definitely beneficial, but it is not nearly sufficient time spent in the Word for our spiritual health. We must be diligent students of the Word daily on our own time. (II Tim. 2:15) Let us develop a greater interest in it. Let us hunger and thirst after its wealth of knowledge. (Matthew 5:6) I guarantee it will show results in your life if it's what you're *most* interested in.

****

A Tale Of Two Influences

"I can make up my own mind." "I have to make my own decisions." "It's nobody else's business but my own." Have you ever had these thoughts before? Have you ever actually voiced these words aloud to someone? Usually these types of things are said when we're trying to defend our actions/behavior to someone – someone who is not agreeing with our actions and behavior! We try to justify things that we know aren't right and that are making our conscience uncomfortable, then convince ourselves that we are solely responsible for ourselves and our actions and that what we do only affects us. But is this really true? Are we the only ones who reap consequences of our behavior? Does it ever affect anyone else? And if so, for how long and to what extent?

I found a very interesting article containing accounts of two different families which I think will illustrate what I'm talking about...

Account 1. Max Jukes was a Dutch settler in New York. He had two sons who married into the same family. These boys' wives came from a family of six daughters. Five of the girls, including the boys' wives, had bad characters. Mr. R. L. Dugdale, appointed to make an investigation of the New York prisons, ran on to this Jukes family. He traced their history for five generations. From these two sons' marriages, this is what he found. Of seven hundred and nine descendants who were investigated, one-fifth of them were criminals, nearly one-fourth were paupers supported at government expense, and about one-fourth of the children were illegitimate. Of the women, one out of six was a prostitute. Dealing with crimes committed by this family cost an estimated one billion three hundred million dollars. And, of course, no one knows the indirect moral and social evil that has sprung from their evil influence.

Account 2. Jonathan Edwards was a minister and a strict disciplinarian in morals. Tracing his genealogical tree, we find twelve college presidents, two hundred sixty-five college graduates, sixty-five college professors, sixty physicians, one hundred ministers, seventy-five army officers, sixty prominent authors, one hundred lawyers, thirty judges, eighty public officers such as governors, mayors, and state officials, three congressmen, two U.S. Senators, and one vice-president of the United States.[1]

As we can see from the above, our influence (bad or good) is far-reaching and long-lasting. I think it is safe to say it has <u>eternal</u> consequences. How many of the Jukes family descendants never knew about the Lord or had the desire to follow Him because of the decisions of two ungodly families years before?

What consequences will be born from the decisions you are making right now in your life? What effect will they have for you, your children, grandchildren, etc.? The poet John Donne once said, "No man is an island entire of itself..." And how true those words are! We are not isolated individuals who can live our lives in such a way that everyone around us remains untouched. Our influence is reaching out, affecting, and determining the future. What tale could be written about your descendants five generations from now...

[1] From *Christian Family* by Dr. Hugo McCord. Copyright 1968 by 20th Century Christian.

****
"...he being dead still speaks." ~Hebrews 11:4
****

"For I have known him, in order that he may command his children and his household after him, that they keep the way of the Lord, to do righteousness and justice..." ~Genesis 18:19
****

"Choose you this day whom you will serve... but as for me and my house, we will serve the Lord." ~Joshua 24:15
****

Oh Be Careful Little Mouth What You Say

These are the words from a children's song sung in Sunday School, but their warning needs to be heeded by adults as well. Words are very powerful and we must choose so carefully the words that we say.

The Bible has much to say about our words and I wanted to share some of these thoughts with you since we women are known to possess the "gift of gab".

Psalm 19:14 says, *"Let the words of my mouth and the meditation of my heart be acceptable in your sight, O Lord, my rock and my redeemer."* We see from this scripture that our words need to be acceptable to the Lord. Christian women should be speaking acceptably every time their mouths open. But what constitutes acceptable speech? One way to answer that question is to look at what kinds of speech are *un*acceptable to the Lord.

*Cursing is unacceptable speech. James 3:10 says, *"Out of the same mouth proceed blessing and cursing, my brethren, these things ought not to be so."*

*Idle and vain words are unacceptable. Matthew 12:36 states, *"But I say to you that for every idle word men may speak, they will give account of it in the day of judgment."*

*Gossip is unacceptable speech. I Timothy 5:13 says, *"And besides they learn to be idle, wandering about from house to house, and not only idle but also gossips and busybodies, saying things which they ought not."*

*Whining and complaining is unacceptable speech. Philippians 2:14 tells us to, *"Do all things without murmuring and complaining."*

*Unkind and ungracious speech is unacceptable. Colossians 4:6 admonishes us, *"Let your speech always be with grace, seasoned with salt..."*

*Angry words are unacceptable. Ephesians 4:26 warns, *"Be angry and sin not."*

*Criticism and discouraging words are unacceptable. Again in Ephesians 4 we are told, *"Let no corrupt communication proceed out of your mouth, but what is good for necessary edification, that it may impart grace to the hearers."* (v. 29)

*Boastful, bragging words are unacceptable. Matthew 6:3,4 says, *"But when you do a charitable deed, do not let your left hand know what your right hand is doing. That your charitable deed may be in secret; and your Father who sees in secret shall reward you openly."*

By examining all of the things which make up unacceptable speech, we can see what words **are** acceptable to the Lord our God: Complimentary words, cheerful words, kind and gracious words, encouraging words and humble words.

If we are having a problem with our speech, we may need to make some changes from within. For the Bible tells us that, *"out of the abundance of the heart, the mouth speaks."* (Matthew 12:34)

Our speech may be one of the hardest things to control, especially if we have formed some bad habits. Gossip, complaining, cursing, criticizing, bragging...all of these are bad habits that must be dealt with and overcome. They don't just hurt others, but ourselves as well.

Our words are so important. Each day we need to think before we speak and weigh carefully the words that we will utter aloud. Jesus has promised us that by our words we will be justified and by our words we will be condemned. (Matthew 12:37) This promise should remind us each and every day to be careful, little mouth, what we say.

****

What Can My Words Do?

-They can tell someone, "Thank You".

-They can encourage someone who is down.

-They can cheer up the sick and lonely.

-They can say, "Congratulations!"

-They can be kind to a hurting soul.

-They can spread laughter to a sad heart.

-They can say, "I love you."

-They can say a prayer.

-They can teach a lost soul about Christ.

****

Be Glad

Have you ever tried playing the "Glad Game"? It's a game where you try to find something to be glad about in every circumstance. Sometimes the game is really hard, but that just makes it more challenging. In Eleanor H. Porter's book, *Pollyanna*, a little orphan girl changes the hearts and minds of an entire town by playing this little game. Pollyanna always looked for something to be glad about in her life and in the lives of those around her. The game originated with her father who was a minister. They were a poor, but happy family. Pollyanna had wanted a doll very badly one time and the church's Ladies Aid Society said they would try to get her one in the next charity barrel that was shipped to the church. As it turned out, there was no doll for her, but only a pair of children's crutches. At first, she cried from disappointment, but her father suggested that they find something to be glad about. They finally concluded that she could be glad that she was healthy and didn't need those crutches! From that day on, they played the "glad game". Even though both of Pollyanna's parents died and she was sent to live with an aunt who really didn't want her, Pollyanna determinedly found something to be glad about each and every day and tried to encourage everyone she met to find a reason to be glad. For example, one lady she met was laid up in bed and had grown bitter about life because of her bedridden circumstance. Pollyanna pointed out that even though she couldn't get out of bed, she could be glad that she could still use her arms and hands to sew and knit and have a usefulness. This little girl had the ability and wisdom at a young age to see the blessings in life, even in the midst of suffering.

Psalm 32:11 states, *"Be glad in the Lord and rejoice, you righteous; and shout for joy, all you upright in heart!"* Psalm 9:2 says, *"I will be glad and rejoice in You; I will sing praise to Your name, O Most High."* Again in Psalm 118:24, *"This is the day that the Lord has made; We will rejoice and be glad in it."* The Scriptures abound with verses such as these that admonish us to be glad and rejoice. We can look around us each day and see the blessings of the Lord in our lives. Not only should this make us glad, but thankful. I Thessalonians 5:18 tells us, *"In everything give thanks..."* When things are good, we should thank and praise God and be glad to have another day in His service. But when things are hard and suffering comes, we do not need to forget to be thankful or to cling to the joy and gladness that comes with a life lived for Jesus. Like Pollyanna, we **can** find something to be glad and thankful about in all things.

Every day of the Christian life needs to be a day of thanksgiving to God our Father for all of the blessings and goodness he bestows and most of all for the salvation we have in Him. It is the very reason that we can be glad.

****

****

Make a joyful shout to the Lord, all you lands!
Serve the Lord with gladness;
Come before His presence with singing.
Know that the Lord, He is God;
It is He who made us, and not we ourselves.
We are His people and the sheep of His pasture.
Enter into His gates with thanksgiving,
And into His courts with praise.
Be thankful to Him, and bless His name.
For the Lord is good;
His mercy is everlasting,
And His truth endures to all generations.
~ Psalm 100

****

Seeing Red

I have been homeschooling my children for 17 years and during that time they have become familiar with an object they call "the dreaded red pen". Every time they take a test or write a report, I use the red pen to mark their papers and show them what is wrong and needs correcting.

In many versions of the Bible today, the words of Jesus are printed in red. Many of His words are teaching and commands we are to follow. They tell us how we need to live our lives in a way that will be pleasing and acceptable to Him. Now some of these teachings are hard – hard enough that they may require some changes on our part.

Generally there are two reactions to the teaching of Jesus: 1) A heart is pricked, godly sorrow is felt, and repentance and obedience follow. (Acts 2:37) Or 2) A heart "sees red" and becomes angry and rebellious to the truth. One example of this is found in Jeremiah chapter 36 when the words of the Lord were given to Jeremiah the prophet to write down in a scroll and then were read before Jehoiakim, the king of Judah. When the scroll was read in the presence of the king, the words of God so enraged him that he took a knife and cut up the scroll and then cast it into the fire (v. 23). Not liking God's Word doesn't change the truth of it. (Incidentally, God had Jeremiah write the same words down in another scroll [v.27,28]. His truth cannot be destroyed!) When we are confronted with the truth of the Bible and we see that some opinions or attitudes we have are not right or there is sin in our lives that needs repenting of, what is our response?

There are many teachings of Jesus that go very counter to our culture today. There are several in the Sermon on the Mount alone (Matthew 5, 6 & 7) such as loving your enemies, being humble, not hating, not seeking vengeance, one scriptural reason for divorce, etc. We need to make sure that we are not embracing worldly ideas and attitudes because we simply don't like or agree with God's stand on the matter. The world's viewpoint on many issues such as abortion, euthanasia, homosexuality and women's role in the church and home is vastly different from God's viewpoint. If we have adopted the world's viewpoint, we need to "get out the red pen" so to speak and start marking the areas of our life that need correction.

When I mark my children's schoolwork with the red pen, they are to see what they did wrong and make the proper corrections so it will then be right.

The words of Jesus are telling us what is right. It is up to us to love Him enough to completely yield our lives to Him in obedience (John 14:15) rather than stiffen our necks in pride and rebellion.

So the next time you open up your Bible to the New Testament, what will your reaction be when you "see red"? Don't let words of correction cause you to be angry or disheartened, but rather let them teach and encourage you to become the kind of Christian woman God wants you to be.

****

Hannah, An Example Of The Power Of Prayer

In the beginning of the book of I Samuel, we read of a woman named Hannah who had a problem. She was married to a man named Elkanah who loved her, but who was also married to another woman named Peninnah. Now, as you can imagine, these two wives did not get along very well at all. In fact, Peninnah (who had many children) would taunt and provoke Hannah who had no children. It was extremely important to Jewish woman to have children and in particular, sons, as they watched and waited for the coming Messiah. To be barren was almost unbearable for these women. This was Hannah's problem; she wanted a child more than anything. Even though the Bible tells us that her husband loved her the most, his love was not enough to cover the ache in her heart over her barren state.

Hannah did the only thing she could do which was the best thing of all: she prayed. Prayer may be defined as a sincere desire of the heart expressed in words; it is the language of faith.

Through Hannah's example, let's look at the four C's of prayer:

1. Cares lead to prayer – Hannah's deep despair drove her to the throne of God, the one true source of comfort and the one source powerful enough to answer. Jonah 2:2 states, *"... I cried out to the Lord because of my affliction, and He answered me."* Jesus pours out his heart in Matthew 26:38 when He says, *"...My soul is exceedingly sorrowful, even to death..."* Hebrews 4:16 encourages us, *"Let us therefore come boldly to the throne of grace, that we may*

obtain mercy and find grace to help in time of need." A quote which sums up the need for prayer in a time of despair states, "Despair can be a blessing, for one attains the noblest heights of spiritual strength on his knees with no one to turn to but God." This is exactly what Hannah did.

2. Command to pray – Prayer is a command as well as a privilege. I Thessalonians 5:17 admonishes us to, *"pray without ceasing"*. James 5:13 asks, *"Is anyone among you suffering? Let him pray."* And Jesus teaches us how to pray beginning in Matthew 6:9, *"In this manner, therefore, pray: Our Father in heaven, hallowed be Your name..."*

3. Conditions of acceptable prayer – We must pray in faith, as Hannah demonstrated. James 1:6 says, *"But let him ask in faith, with no doubting, for he who doubts is like a wave of the sea driven and tossed by the wind."* Ask with the right motive. James 4:3 warns, *"You ask and do not receive, because you ask amiss, that you may spend it on your pleasures."* We need to pray in harmony with God's will. In I John 5:14 we're told, *"Now this is the confidence that we have in Him, that if we ask anything according to His will, He hears us."*

4. Comfort of prayer – After Hannah had poured out her heart and petition to God, we're told in I Samuel 1:18 that she, *"...went her way and ate, and her face was no longer sad."* Jesus promises in Matthew 11:28, *"Come to me, all you who labor and are heavy laden, and I will give you rest."* And we're encouraged by the words of I

Peter 5:7, *"casting all your care upon Him, for He cares for you."*

Hannah's cares led her to pray. She did as commanded and prayed in an acceptable way which led to her being comforted. God heard and answered the desire of her heart by blessing her with a son which she named Samuel. Hannah says in I Samuel 1:27, *"For this child I prayed, and the Lord has granted me my petition which I asked of Him."* And what do you think the name Samuel means? "Asked of God."

****

P – Praise

R – Reflect

A – Ask

Y – Yield

****

A Contented Life

We are a nation of discontent. Just watch the television commercials that tell us the cars we drive, the televisions we watch, the clothes we wear, and the houses we live in are not nearly good enough. We need something bigger and better! What about implications through popular television shows and books that you can't possibly be happy with your spouse when there's so many other appealing fish in the sea? All of these messages are geared to making us feel discontent with what we have. Perhaps it makes us feel restless, unhappy or even downright depressed because we think we don't have what we "need".

Unfortunately, this attitude has even made its way into the church. There are Christians who are very discontented with their lives. Maybe its their finances, marriages, marital status or lack of material things. We know this kind of attitude is not pleasing to God, so if we're guilty of having it, how can we change it to being happy and content in this life?

First, we need to understand that *true contentment is not based on outward circumstances.* If we let our happiness and contentment depend solely on what's going on in our lives, then we've missed the mark. We'll never reach that level of contentment we're striving for because it's not found in anything worldly.

Second, *contentment has to be learned.* Again, it does not depend on outward circumstances, but rather it depends on our mind and heart accepting our circumstances for what they are and learning to be content in spite of them. It is not an automatic feeling, but one that we cultivate.

Third, *a contented heart is one that is thankful.* When we truly have a heart full of thankfulness to God for all that we do have and all that He has done for us, we will not have room for the lurkings of discontent.

Now these things do not depend on our strength alone, but through Christ we can have the strength to overcome the attitude of discontentment and learn to be happy and fulfilled in the life God blesses us with.

The apostle Paul sums it all up so well in Philippians 4:11-13 where he said, *"Not that I speak in regard to need, for I have learned in whatever state I am, to be content: I know how to be abased and how to abound. Everywhere and in all things I have learned both to be full and to be hungry, both to abound and to suffer need. I can do all things through Christ who strengthens me."* Paul had experienced both sides of the coin. He knew what it was like to have plenty and what it was like to suffer need. Yet he was content with either situation because he was strengthened and sustained by Christ.

I once read the following statement which makes a lot of sense: "When we look at what we want and then compare that with what we have, we shall be unhappy. When we think of what we deserve, then of what we have, we shall thank God." Always pining for what someone else has renders us unthankful and impotent because we waste time sorrowing over what we can't have instead of using our life as it is in service to God.

Maybe your finances are tight, maybe your house isn't as big or nice as someone else's, maybe you're single and wish you were married, maybe you're married and wish you were single. Stop dwelling on what isn't and be thankful to God for your very life, for the gift of salvation and for providing you with what you absolutely need to live. Look at your life through His perspective and see all of the blessings in it and opportunities He gives you. Fill your heart with thankfulness, leaving no room for discontent. Focus on the good things God gives and does for you. Realize that the Lord is all that you absolutely need and don't look to external circumstances to provide contentment. Don't focus on the life that you *don't* have and end up missing out on the life that you *do* have. Strengthen yourself through Christ and feel the joy of a contented life in Him.

****

The Serenity Prayer

Lord, help me to accept the things I cannot change; to change the things I can, and the wisdom to know the difference.

****

Speaking Without Words

For my birthday last week, one of my children gave me a cute card that said, "Here's a handy guide to a mother's many facial expressions and what they mean". The card then proceeded to show 9 different facial expressions and gave a translation for each of them. My favorite was #7 – The Sideways Warning Glance – which means you'd better change the subject before you embarrass the whole family in front of company! We all laughed as we read the card and realized the truth of it. There are many faces a mother can make at her children and they get the message loud and clear without her having to say one word!

We have probably all heard the saying that "actions speak louder than words". Let's consider that thought. A husband or wife may tell their spouse, "I love you" daily, but consistently show something different through their actions. Being selfish by putting their own wants and needs ahead of their spouse day after day will speak volumes and render the words, "I love you" meaningless. It is the same in any other relationship as well. Friends will no longer consider you a true friend when you say one thing and constantly do another. Your children will not have the proper respect for you if you are "teaching" them by telling them not to do something that you yourself do in front of them all of the time. They are not stupid, they see the hypocrisy. It is important to say the right things to our spouses, friends, and children, but more importantly, we need to back up those words with the right actions.

What are we communicating to God? Whether we realize it or not, we are all "telling" God how we feel about Him even when we say nothing. Jesus said in Matthew 7:21, *"Not everyone who says to Me, 'Lord, Lord' shall enter the kingdom of heaven, but he who does the will of my Father in heaven."* He further states in John 14:15, *"If you love Me, keep My commandments."* Notice that Jesus is not interested in lip service. The real test of our love for Him is by the service we are rendering through our actions. Over and over in the scriptures, it is stated to do, to obey, to work, to keep the commandments, etc. God places an emphasis on **action**. It is an easy thing to say with our mouths: "I am a Christian", "I believe in God", "I love the Lord", "I want to go to heaven", but a harder thing to show it by faithfully living for Him each minute and doing His will. How do you "tell" God that you believe in Him, that you love Him with all of your heart, and that you desire to do His will without saying it in words? Are you faithfully studying the scriptures, loving others as yourself, raising your children in the nurture and admonition of the Lord, forsaking not the assembly of the saints, serving…? Your day to day actions speak volumes to the Lord. If you are not doing God's will then you are telling God something – that He is really not all that important to you regardless of what your words say.

On my birthday card, the first look was the "penetrating stare" which meant that mother was reading your mind. What does God see as He stares into our heart and lives? What are we telling God without even saying a word?

****

Think On These Things

"*Finally, brethren, whatever things are true, whatever things are noble, whatever things are just, whatever things are pure, whatever things are lovely, whatever things are of good report, if there is any virtue and if there is anything praiseworthy – think on these things.*" (Philippians 4:8) These words that came from the pen of Paul and the mouth of God should be ones that we have committed to memory. They serve as an instructional daily guide as to what kinds of things we as Christians should listen to, watch, speak, and think about.

Romans 12:2 teaches us that we are not to be conformed to this world, but transformed by the *renewing of our minds*. Christians do not think the same way that the world thinks. If we ever question if reading a certain book is okay or if listening to certain music, watching a certain show, participating in a certain activity, etc. is okay, all we have to do is to apply Philippians 4:8 and see if it passes the test. Is it something pure, noble, or full of virtue? No problem then! But if we can't honestly say that it is, then we need to make the proper decision concerning it.

Years ago there was a popular saying regarding computers: Garbage In, Garbage Out. That can certainly apply to our minds. If we continually feed our minds garbage through what we read, watch, and listen to, what do we expect will be manifested in our hearts? In Matthew 12:34, Jesus says, "*How can you speak good, when you are evil? For out of the abundance of the heart, the mouth speaks.*" What we say and do is a reflection of the condition of our hearts; whether they be spiritually healthy or corrupt. The condition of our hearts is in turn a reflection of what we have put into it – garbage or pure things.

As a parent, there have been certain things through the years that I have forbidden my children to participate in or read or listen to. I have never done this in order to make their lives miserable or to make them unpopular with their peers. I have done it because I knew that certain things were "garbage" and were not profitable spiritually to them. Let me urge you who are parents to be very mindful of what your children are reading, watching and listening to. Don't just take their word for it that it's "okay" or "not that bad" or "everyone else is reading it, watching it, etc." Check it out for yourselves and see if it passes the Philippians 4:8 test.

God as our Father does the same for us. He doesn't forbid things to make our lives miserable; rather, He knows what is beneficial for us in every aspect of our lives and if we will submit to His will, we will have pure hearts and lives that can truly serve Him, and in so doing, we will live the happiest lives of all people on the earth.

Why not try memorizing and applying Philippians 4:8 to help us all to feed our hearts with the good and pure things God gives us through His word, thereby renewing our minds as we "*think on these things*".

****

"Thy word have I hid in mine heart that I might not sin against thee." ~Psalm 119:105

****

Code Adam

"Code Adam, repeat, we have a Code Adam. Three year old girl wearing a pink Minnie Mouse dress. Blue eyes, light brown hair in a ponytail." I stood there in shock as I listened to a Wal-Mart employee announce a description over the intercom of my little girl, Hannah. Hannah was lost. I had been shopping with my three children on that Saturday afternoon and had already gone through the checkout with my purchases. I stopped at the front of the store to look at a display of telescopes with my oldest son. I don't know how long I looked; it seemed to be just a moment. When I turned to continue on toward the door, I couldn't find my daughter anywhere. It seemed she had vanished into thin air. With a panicked feeling, I looked all around and then started grabbing people and asking them if they'd seen my little girl. An employee noticed how frantic I was getting and she asked if I lost a child. As soon as I said yes, she got a quick description and announced it over the intercom.

Wal-Mart stores, as well as some other national chain stores, have a system they employ to find lost children in their stores. It is called "Code Adam" and it is named after a little boy, Adam Walsh, who was abducted from a store several years ago. When a Code Adam is announced, the employees are immediately supposed to be on the lookout for the lost child. Someone checks the bathrooms, the fitting rooms, and some will even run into the parking lot to start scanning the crowd. They continue to search and repeat the description over the intercom at intervals until the child is found.

After what seemed an eternity to me, an employee of

the optical department walked over to me with a little three year old girl in her pink Minnie Mouse dress by the name of Hannah Marilyn Pryor. I can't begin to describe how I felt to see my little girl safe and back with her mother! As I profusely thanked the employees, I heard them announce, "Cancel Code Adam". This means that the lost child had been found.

How many "Code Adam's" do you think the Lord still has active right now? How many children of our Father are out there in the world, lost? He can tell you their physical descriptions right down to the number of hairs on their heads. He is waiting and watching for them to return to the safety of his arms. Are His "employees" out searching? Do we heed the message getting announced at intervals that there are lost ones we need to look for?

What would I as a parent have thought of a Wal-Mart employee who ignored the Code Adam announcement about Hannah? Maybe they even saw her and didn't bother to report it or bring her back. Maybe they were too busy going on their break. Or they might have figured that someone else would find her eventually and take care of her. I would have been extremely angry and hurt had I known. Why would someone delay my anxiety and heartache by not bringing her back to me?

Do we delay God's heartache over the lost by not bringing them to Him? Do we have any neighbors, friends, co-workers, or family members that are lost? I hope and pray that we might show the diligence and concern that those store employees showed for my child.

I would like to address three different groups. First, if you have never known God as your heavenly Father by obeying the gospel and becoming a Christian, I pray that you will do so today. If you need to know how, you may email me at *heatherpryor@knology.net* for assistance. Second, if you are a child of God who has strayed away from your Father, please come back to Him today. He has been waiting for this very thing. And third, if you are not lost yourself, please consider your diligence in finding others who are lost. Don't become too busy or apathetic to ignore those lost souls right out there under your own nose. There is a Father depending on you to do your job by finding them and restoring them.

As I took my little daughter out to the car, I hugged her tight as my tears fell. I was so thankful to the Lord for restoring her back to me. How much more does the Lord Himself feel when we bring a lost one back to Him! The Bible tells us there is much rejoicing in heaven over the lost one that is found. How wonderful it would be to say regarding that precious soul, "Cancel Code Adam, the one that was lost is now found."

****

Learning (and Loving) To Teach

In homeschooling my children for the past fourteen years, I have noticed something. I have a lot more enthusiasm as a teacher when I am teaching a subject I am interested in and have knowledge about. For example, I majored in English in college so I can diagram a sentence like nobody's business and identify gerunds, infinitives and predicate nominatives until the cows come home. It's fun for me and easy for me to teach. I also happen to love literature and literary analysis. I enjoy reading books with my children and discussing things like theme, conflict, and onomatopoeia (look that one up if you don't know it. :)) History is an enjoyable subject and one of great interest to me as well. I have no trouble teaching these subjects and showing enthusiasm about them because I like them and have knowledge concerning them. Math and science on the other hand... well, suffice it to say I have to struggle with teaching these to my kids because I don't like them myself, and I really don't have much knowledge in these areas. (This is where teachers on DVD really come in handy!) All of this leads me to wonder if the same isn't true concerning our teaching others the gospel. Could it be that we don't do it because we don't feel knowledgeable about the Bible and/or we don't have a lot of enthusiasm about the subject? And if so, what can we do to change that?

First of all, we need to have knowledge concerning the Bible. There is only one way to do this and that is to get into the Word and do plenty of reading and study on a daily basis. It is true that there is benefit in listening to sermons and Bible classes, but there is no substitute for the amount of knowledge you will gain if you engage in a serious course of personal daily Bible study. Sometimes in studying the Bible, you will have more questions than answers, but that is a good thing. These questions should drive us even deeper and further into God's Word. Jesus said in Matthew 5:6, *"Blessed are those who hunger and thirst for righteousness, for they shall be filled."* David stated in the very first Psalm about the blessed or happy man that, *"...his delight is in the law of the Lord, and in His law he meditates day and night."* The apostle Peter admonished Christians to *"desire the pure milk of the word, that you may grow thereby"* (I Peter 2:2) and also to *"grow in the grace and knowledge of our Lord and Savior Jesus Christ."* (II Peter 3:18)

The second part of the equation is to have enthusiasm about the knowledge we have. Our walk with the Lord, our love of His word, and desire to do His will above all things will drive us to be enthusiastic teachers and sharers of the gospel. Satan tries to tempt us with so many things to distract us from our Christianity as well as try to make us feel bored and apathetic about the Lord, His church and His work. We need to "light the fires in our souls" as the song says and get excited about what God has done for us and in turn what He can do for others. Psalm 32:11 tells us, *"Be glad in the Lord and rejoice, you righteous, and shout for joy, all you upright in heart!"* David also states in Psalm 122:1, *"I was glad when they said to me, 'Let us go into the house of the Lord.'"* We need to truly feel the joy there is in worshiping our Lord and serving Him.

Let us all strive harder to work on our knowledge of God's Word and our ability to share it as well as being happy, joyful and enthusiastic Christians. We have such a responsibility as teachers where a diploma is not at stake, but souls are.

****

Here's a little test of your Bible knowledge to get you started. Which book of the Bible on the left contains the descriptions on the right? Good luck!

1. Acts   a. Paul's presentation of what Christians believe
2. Exodus   b. Prophecies about the Messiah
3. Genesis   c. Songs of praise, requests for help
4. Isaiah   d. Story of beginnings of the earth
5. Joshua   e. Story of Jesus' life and death
6. Matthew   f. Story of the early church
7. Proverbs   g. Story of the Israelites' entry into Canaan
8. Psalms   h. Story of the Israelites' flight out of Egypt
9. Revelation   i. Visions of John
10. Romans   j. Wise sayings

Answers on page 137

****

Is Your Diffuser Working?

Essential oils are a popular trend these days. Just search the internet and you will find countless links for using essential oils, as wells as individuals and companies that offer them for sale. There are a large variety of oils available on the market today and all of them have a fragrance: some are pleasant, some are strong, and some are somewhat disagreeable. For instance, some of my favorite oil scents are lavender, geranium, orange, and lemon while others such as clary sage and tea tree tend to make me wrinkle my nose. One of the ways in which these oils can be used is to put them into a diffuser which breaks down the molecules of the oil and disperses it into the air. The scent is inhaled and stimulates the brain for such things as relaxation, concentration, or a sense of well-being. These oil diffusers work by permeation, electricity and heat. Interestingly enough, we too act as a diffuser.

In II Corinthians 2:14-15 the apostle Paul says, *"Now thanks be to God who always leads us in triumph in Christ, and **through us diffuses the fragrance of His knowledge in every place**. For we are to God the fragrance of Christ among those who are being saved and among whose who are perishing."* (NKJV) Each one of us is to be diffusing the fragrance of Christ. We are to be dispersing that fragrance of the knowledge of God everywhere that we go. In order to do that, our diffuser has to work much like the oil diffuser does.

- **Permeation** – How can we begin to diffuse the fragrance of God's knowledge if we don't first possess it ourselves? The oil diffuser won't have anything to disperse if it is not first filled up with the proper essential oils. We need to study, learn, and grow in the grace and knowledge of God's Word, filling ourselves to the brim so it will overflow to others. Ephesians 3:19 tells us, *"To know the love of Christ which passes knowledge; that you may be filled with all the fullness of God."*

- **Electricity** – In order for the oil diffuser to do its job, it must be plugged into a power source. Jesus Christ is our power source and it is through Him and His strength that we are able to accomplish His will. Philippians 4:13 reminds us, *"I can do all things through Christ who strengthens me."* If we aren't plugged in to the proper power source, our diffuser will not work.

- **Heat** – After the oil diffuser is turned on, the oils inside of it are slowly heated until they reach the proper temperature to be released into the air. If we are a lukewarm Christian or a flat-out cold one, we will never have enough heat to diffuse the fragrance of Christ to the world around us. As the song says, we must "Light the fire!" in our hearts and burn inside not only for the word of God but for the opportunity to share it and the desire to do His will each day.

The fragrance of Christ that we are diffusing to others, will have an effect either positive or negative. Continuing on in II Corinthians 2:16, *"To the one, we are the aroma of death to death, and to the other the aroma of life to life."* Just as some of the essential oils are not pleasant to smell, so some in the world will be repelled by the fragrance of Christ and the knowledge of him. However, others will find it a welcoming and pleasing scent that they will be drawn to and want more of. Our mission is not to make people like the fragrance of Christ; that is entirely up to them. Our job is simply to be the diffusers of that fragrance as God wants us to be.

Is your diffuser working? Are you permeated with the word of God, filling yourself with its knowledge? Are you plugged into the proper power source and drawing your strength from Jesus Christ? Are you on fire for God and cultivating a burning desire to serve Him each day? If not, now is a good time to get your diffuser in working order so that the fragrance of His knowledge can be dispersed in every place.

****

The First Five Minutes

At a ladies seminar, the question was asked, "How many of you have had your feelings hurt by a sister within the first five minutes of walking in the church building?" In a room full of over 300 women, hands immediately shot up everywhere. How sad. I was present at that seminar and the question (along with its subsequent response) made me stop and think about how we should be conducting ourselves beginning the minute we arrive at the Lord's house of worship. Let's consider some things we should/should not do in the first five minutes...

When we arrive on Sunday morning, many of us have a mental "To Do" list buzzing in our heads that is bursting to get out of our mouths the second we're inside. But let's take a minute and consider – if we're asking a teacher, elder, or preacher to do something, we may be distracting them. Many times, they are trying to center their minds on the lesson they are about to present and it is very disturbing to them to be sidetracked the second their foot crosses the threshold. Instead, let's spend the first five minutes greeting them and encouraging them in their teaching. The "To Do" list can wait until after services or be asked of someone else who is not preparing to teach.

When we walk in and see a visitor, do we spend the first five minutes avoiding them, doing other "important" things, or do we immediately go to welcome them and introduce ourselves?

When we walk in and immediately see an erring member that has finally returned to the fold, do we spend the first five minutes greeting them sarcastically or snubbing them coldly? Instead, how about we warmly welcome them home.

In the first five minutes, do we flock to our family and friends to the exclusion of fellowshiping with others? It can be a real challenge to break out of our comfort zone to strike up a conversation with someone we're not too familiar with, but it gets easier with time and practice. Make it a point to talk to someone new at each service.

How about spending the first five minutes encouraging instead of tearing down, complimenting instead of criticizing, and loving instead of hurting? What a difference it would make in our fellowship and in our worship.

As I write this, I am challenging myself first and foremost. How do I spend my first five minutes in the church building? Are my words, actions and heart pleasing to God in those moments? If they haven't been, I pray they now will be.

I believe the key to this is in preparing our hearts before we ever arrive. We need to have our minds focused on the Lord and our worship of Him, cultivating a proper attitude of humility before Him, giving thanks to God for His blessings and the opportunity to worship and fellowship with our spiritual family. If we will do this, we should arrive with a smile on our face, God's peace in our hearts, and a proper attitude toward worship and others.

I challenge all of my Christian sisters to be more mindful of how we are spending the first five minutes.

****

Bored By The Bible?

What is your favorite book? Is it an adventure novel, a romance, or perhaps a classic work of literature that has withstood the test of time? Think about what makes the book so appealing to you. Perhaps you like the setting of the book and its vivid descriptions of beautiful scenery, or maybe it has a fascinating main character or an exciting plot line.

Our favorite books are ones that we like to read over and over. We practically have them memorized and have certain scenes in them that we never tire of reading and experiencing. They have become a familiar friend.

The Bible is the best-selling book of all time with Guinness World Records estimating that over 5 billion copies have been sold. Yet, of the millions of people that own a copy of this best-seller, how many would say it is their favorite book?

Why are so many people (even Christians) bored by the Bible? Perhaps they see it as a disjointed collection of writings that are put together without any seeming cohesion, or they try reading it like a novel and soon get overwhelmed by the growing cast of characters and events that seem to have nothing to do with each other and they get bogged down and lost. They can't make any sense of it as they read it and it soon goes by the wayside, doomed to sit on a shelf along with their other unread books.

What if we looked at the Bible differently? What if we understood that the Bible is one book made up of 66 chapters with one author – God. What if we realized that His book is telling one story: the story of redemption through His Son Jesus Christ. He weaves that consistent thread through each and every "chapter" of His book. He starts at the very beginning of time with the history of the world and mankind. Very early on, we read of the severing of man's relationship with God due to sin and the hope that God immediately holds out through the promise of a coming Savior. We see the continued efforts of Satan to thwart God's plan, his near successes, and his ultimate failure. Along the way, we are introduced to some fascinating characters who went through some extraordinary experiences and teach us many things through their examples, both good and bad. They are numerous tiny threads that are interwoven in this story and they all have a connection to its ultimate theme. For example, when we read about foreign kings and nations who would fight against Israel, subject them to slavery, or take them captive, we need to realize that *"God rules in the kingdoms of men"* (Daniel 4:17) and is the One orchestrating all of these events according to His plan. We also see this as He uses foreign rulers and events to bring about a good result. God told Isaiah the prophet to write about Cyrus who would be used as God's instrument to orchestrate the rebuilding of the temple in Jerusalem by the Jews after they returned from exile in Babylonian captivity. We are first introduced to King Cyrus in Isaiah 44:28 when the prophecy about him was made 150 years before he ascended to the Persian throne. We read about the fulfillment of the prophecy in the book of Ezra. When we connect the dots of the people and events in the Bible, it does make sense, and it is fascinating and compelling reading. It is amazing to see the hand of God in control of all things and the way He brings about His master plan.

If you want to develop a greater interest in the Bible, it will require a few things:

- **Attitude.** Have a proper attitude of reverence for its author, almighty God, and a profound appreciation for the words of salvation that are offered to us on its pages. It's the most important book we can ever read; we need to keep that in mind with an attitude of gratitude every time we open its pages.

- **Diligence.** Reading the Bible takes work – hard work. It is not "fast food" literature but a full course meal that takes time to chew on and digest. Reading it means studying it. When you read a word you don't understand, look it up right then. Check cross references to make connections. Do some research into people or events or cultural meanings that give you more background information and a deeper understanding of what you're reading. Look for life applications, both to the people it was written to at the time and to us today. Read the Bible to grow spiritually and to learn!

- **Atmosphere.** It's difficult to get much out of Bible reading when you're surrounded by TV, music, or other distractions. Find a quiet place and choose a quiet time for serious reading and study. Allow yourself to become 100% engaged and absorbed in your reading. Don't rush through it; give yourself plenty of time to reap the full benefits.

- **Frequency.** Bible reading isn't to be done when you finally have some free time with nothing else to do. The more you read it, the more familiar you become with it and the more skillful you will be in utilizing it. Let it become your familiar friend.

Bored by the Bible? The Bible is anything *but* boring. It is the greatest book of all time, written by the greatest author with the greatest message. Be excited by it and delve deeply into its pages. Be thankful for the privilege of holding such a treasure in your hands.

****

"I rejoice at your word as one who finds great treasure." ~Psalm 119:162

"The law of the Lord is perfect, reviving the soul; the testimony of the Lord is sure, making wise the simple; the precepts of the Lord are right, rejoicing the heart; the commandment of the Lord is pure, enlightening the eyes; the fear of the Lord is clean, enduring forever; the rules of the Lord are true and righteous altogether. More to be desired are they than gold, even much fine gold; sweeter also than honey and drippings of the honeycomb." ~Psalm 119:7-10

****

Christian Womanhood & Family

Could God Have Chosen You?

He was searching for just the right one. He was looking for someone with a tender and loving heart. One who was thoughtful, compassionate, and totally unselfish. She needed to be someone whose heart and soul were totally dedicated to God and who would be faithful in raising her children to love and serve the Lord. This couldn't be just any woman; she needed to be very special because He was choosing her for an extraordinary job – to be the mother of the Savior of the world.

God chose Mary to be the mother of Jesus Christ, the Messiah. What a tremendous privilege – and heavy responsibility. As He searched the hearts of the women at that time very carefully to find just the right one to raise His son and our Savior, what must He have seen in Mary's heart? We are given some insight into her character when the angel Gabriel first appears to her. He greets Mary as the *"highly favored one"* and tells her that she is *"blessed among women"* (Luke 1:28). To emphasize the point again, he tells her that she *"found favor with God."* (Luke 1:30) Gabriel is letting Mary know that she was not just randomly selected for this undertaking, she was specially selected. God was choosing just the right one in choosing Mary as Jesus' mother.

We see Mary's humility, unselfishness, and great faith revealed to us as she listens to Gabriel's message and willingly embraces God's plan for her. She may not understand everything about it and probably has many questions swirling about in her head, but the bottom line is in her answer as she says to the angel, *"Behold the maidservant of the Lord! Let it be to me according to your word."* (Luke 1:38) Mary loved and trusted God. She believed in Him, and was totally submissive to Him with a heart full of faith.

We see the normal concerns of a mother in Mary as Jesus grew up. She was naturally distressed and anxious when Jesus went missing for three days when he was twelve years old. (Luke 3:41-50) She trusted in Jesus' wisdom and judgment as the Messiah when she appealed to him for help at the wedding feast in Cana (John 2:10), and she stood at the foot of a cross bearing her son watching in pain and agony as her mother heart broke.

There is not much more information we are given about Mary, but I think it is safe to say that we could make a few assumptions about her based on the very fact that God chose her. I think she probably would have fit the mold of the virtuous woman in Proverbs 31 pretty well. Would you picture Mary as industrious or lazy? Would you think she provided well for her household or just did her own thing leaving her family to fend for themselves? Do you think she spoke with kindness and gentleness or was shrill, bossy, or harsh? Could the heart of her husband Joseph safely trust in her or was he always uneasy as to what she was doing behind his back? Would Jesus and his siblings have been able to *"rise up and call her blessed"* (Proverbs 31:28)? Was Mary a woman who could be praised because she feared the Lord? I think the answers to all of these questions are obvious. Mary's sterling character, beautiful heart, and dedicated faith are blatantly obvious to us because God chose her. Was she perfect? No, but she was pliable. She was willing to be molded by God into what He wanted and needed her to be. God was not interested in a mother for His son who was selfish, lazy, unkind, ungrateful, or lukewarm in her faith. He chose a woman who had all of the qualities that first and foremost made her a pleasing daughter to her heavenly Father. Once that foundation was established in her heart, it just naturally followed that she would make an excellent mother for Jesus Christ the Lord.

My question is – could God have chosen you? Could God have chosen me? If God had been looking for a mother for his son, the Savior of the world, during this time in history, what would He see in each of us? Could we have passed that crucial test? Do we have a beautiful character like Mary? Do we have an unselfish heart like hers? Most importantly, do we have a strong faith and unwavering dedication to God like she had? Could God have chosen you?

****

Having A Mary Heart In A Martha World

What kind of world do we as women live in today? It is one that is filled with many activities, responsibilities, and demands on our time – you know, all of those things that we simply **must** do. I call it a "Martha" world. Keep reading to see what I mean:

"Now it happened as they went that He entered a certain village; and a certain woman named Martha welcomed Him into her house. And she had a sister called Mary, who also sat at Jesus' feet and heard His word. But Martha was distracted with much serving, and she approached Him and said, 'Lord, do You not care that my sister has left me to serve alone? Therefore tell her to help me.' And Jesus answered and said to her, 'Martha, Martha, you are worried and troubled about many things. But one thing is needed, and Mary has chosen that good part, which will not be taken away from her.'" Luke 10:38-42

Notice what Martha was <u>not</u> doing in this passage. She wasn't doing anything evil or wicked. She wasn't being lazy. She wasn't being rude. In fact, she was being quite industrious and hospitable by preparing a meal for Jesus. And yet, Jesus chides Martha. Why? He was not condemning hard work or hospitality by any means, but rather He wanted Martha to realize that she was being distracted with all of her "must do" things. We are told nothing which indicates that Mary was lazy and left her sister to do all of the work all of the time, but we are told that Mary had made a wise choice in realizing what was truly important: Jesus. Mary knew that taking the time to be with Jesus and feeding on the spiritual food was more important right then than a physical meal.

Now, if you're a "Martha", raise your hand! Yes, I see many of you out there. I tend to be one myself. Again, there is nothing wrong with working hard and staying busy, but we can't let that distract us from what is truly important. Our "busyness" becomes a problem when it interferes with our time and service to the Lord. We should fit our schedules around the Lord; not fit the Lord around our schedules. For example, are we skipping church services because we have "so many things to do!" Do days go by without our uttering a single prayer? How many days a week (if any) are we reading and studying our Bibles? Maybe we neglect to make a phone call or visit or send a card of encouragement because we really don't have the time to spare. If this is the case, we need to make some adjustments. The Lord has **never** been too busy for us; God forbid we should ever say we are too busy to have any time for Him.

In reading this, I hope that we will all strive to have a heart more like Mary's. Focus on "choosing that good part" of devoting our time and energy to the Lord first. We live in a Martha world and that will never change, but the focus of our hearts and actions can change. Have a Mary heart!

****

Take Time To Be Holy

Take time to be holy, speak oft with thy Lord;
Abide in Him always, and feed on His Word;
Make friends of God's children, help those who are weak;
Forgetting in nothing His blessing to seek.

Take time to be holy, the world rushes on;
Spend much time in secret with Jesus alone;
By looking to Jesus, like Him thou shalt be;
Thy friends in thy conduct His likeness shall see.

Take time to be holy, let Him by thy Guide
And run not before Him, whatever betide;
In joy or in sorrow, still follow the Lord;
And looking to Jesus, still trust in His word.

Take time to be holy, be calm in thy soul;
Each tho't and each motive beneath His control;
Thus led by His Spirit to fountains of love,
Thou soon shall be fitted for service above.

~W. D. Longstaff

Gifts Of Motherhood

As Mother's Day is approaching, I have been thinking about some of the gifts I've received over the years from my three children. As I started to compile the mental list, I went way beyond Mother's Day. Here's a look at some of the "gifts" on my list:

- Months of morning sickness, heartburn, and back pain
- Nights with little to no sleep
- A gallon (or pretty close) of spitup running down my dress as I was all ready to leave for church
- Diapers full of what might be classified as toxic waste
- Fingerprints on the walls
- Dirty footprints on the floor
- Terrible 2's (times three)
- The serenade of siblings yelling and fighting in the midst of a headache
- Days of polishing my math skills as I made calculations as to how many years, months, weeks, days, and seconds till they're all grown up
- The indescribable feeling of holding my baby for the first time (times three)
- The first smile of each of my children
- Seeing them take their first steps, speak their first word, and all of the other wonderful "firsts"

- Feeling chubby toddler arms hug my neck
- Getting wet kisses on my cheek from my one-year-old
- Bouquets of wildflowers picked with a little girl's hands
- Hearing them read a book all by themselves for the first time
- Listening to them pray
- Seeing them receive awards and achievements that make me proud
- Watching them all play nicely together
- Hearing them recite Bible verses
- Hearing their laughter
- Seeing them be helpful without asking
- Hearing the song, "Jesus Loves Me" sung from a little preschooler's heart
- Seeing them smile at me as I hear them say, "I love you, Mom"

I am looking forward to many more gifts as the years go by. I can't wait to receive the gifts of seeing them graduate, getting married, having children of their own, and most importantly, the tremendous gift of seeing each and every one of them become a Christian. I've received so many things as a mother and still have so many more to come. But the greatest gifts I've received as a mother are the ones God gave me Himself: Nicholas, Hannah and Matthew.

****

****

"For this child I prayed, and the Lord has granted me the petition of my heart which I asked of Him."

~I Samuel 1:27

****

*Postscript: Since first publishing the above article, I have seen some of my wishes come true. So far, I have seen my two oldest graduate and best of all, I have seen all three of them become Christians. God is so good!

Are You A Titus 2 Woman?

"...the older women likewise, that they be reverent in behavior, not slanderers, not given to much wine, teachers of good things – that they admonish the young women to love their husbands, to love their children, to be discreet, chaste, homemakers, good, obedient to their own husbands, that the word of God may not be blasphemed." Titus 2:3-5

The book of Titus was written by the apostle Paul to a young preacher named Titus. Paul was giving Titus some advice on setting the church in Crete in order. (1:5) He starts by telling him to appoint qualified elders. (1:5-9) Chapter 2 is an "instruction manual" for Titus to follow in teaching the rest of the church, the body of members, how they should conduct themselves. He doesn't leave anyone out. Older men, older women, younger women and even servants are all covered in this chapter. Each person, male or female, young or old has specific teachings directed to him concerning his role in the church and in his life. Let's look at the teachings given to women.

Paul breaks it down into two categories: older women and younger women. (I'll let you decide for yourself which category you fit into!) The instructions are very clear as to the role of older Christian women. They are to be **teachers**. To whom? The younger women. Of what? Good things and their role in the home. Now Paul qualifies this by saying that these women who ought to be teaching the younger women should be ones who are reverent, not slanderers (don't run their mouths with gossip and negative comments about other people), and ones who will teach the doctrines of the Lord and not their own ideas and opinions.

There are many broken and unhappy homes in the church today. There are many reasons for this, but one of which is we don't have significant numbers of godly, older Christian women teaching and mentoring the younger women at all or not in the teachings of God concerning the home. I've heard some older women preaching the worldly, feminist doctrines of careers over family, independence, and non-submission. That is not what the Bible teaches a Christian woman to be like and that is <u>not</u> what the older women are commanded to teach the younger. Sometimes, there is also an attitude among older women that they have "put in their time" and any teaching that needs to be done should be passed on to the younger women. That is contrary to scripture. Chapter 2, verses 3 and 4 give clear instructions to the **older** women to teach and admonish the younger. How are the younger women supposed to teach themselves how to love their husbands and children and how to be a good homemaker if they don't have the experience and wisdom to do so? They need the example of wise, experienced, older Christian women who have raised faithful children, had long, successful marriages, and made a happy Christ-centered home for their families.

Now for the younger women we turn to verses 4 and 5 of chapter 2. There are a number of things we are to learn from the older women. We are to be good listeners to the wisdom of our older sisters in Christ and then put into practice the teachings we have received. These teachings are the words of the Lord and they consist of: loving our husbands and being obedient and submissive to them, loving our children, being discreet, chaste (modest), being homemakers, and being good. To some this sounds like a tall or virtually impossible order to fill. But ladies, this is God's design for the role of women in the home and the church and we know that God does not make mistakes; He is not wrong. He set up the church and the home and the roles of men and women specifically. When His design is followed, there is order, peace and happiness. It is when we tamper with this design that things don't go so smoothly. It is a joy to love our husbands and children in the way that God intended. It is a joy to make our homes a happy place for our families. I have heard it said that the woman is the emotional hub of the wheel that makes up the home. The husband and children are the spokes that revolve around her. If she has a rotten attitude, it rubs off on her family. Contrast that with a woman who has made her home a haven for her family and who is the cheerful, loving center of it. Her family gravitates to her like insects around a light in the darkness. Your role as an obedient Christian woman, whether older or younger is so important. It makes all of the difference to your family and church. Ask yourself in all honesty and humility, "Am I the Titus 2 woman God wants me to be?" Don't cling to the false teachings of the world concerning a "happy, fulfilled woman". Be truly fulfilled by filling your God-given role.

****

What Gifts Will You Give Your Children?

As Christmas day approaches, everyone starts contemplating what gifts to get for the special children in their lives. Most children make a list of things that they really, really want for Christmas and don't we try as hard as we can to get them those things they want most? Sometimes they can't have everything on their list because it's too costly or it's something that is liable to break easily or it's not age appropriate. But we strive to give them things that are special and that they'll get lasting enjoyment from.

Would you like some of the very best gift suggestions? Gifts that never wear out or need exchanging, ones that fit every child and that are priceless? Let's take a look at some of these gifts we can give our children:

1) The gift of TIME - I have observed some children who had plenty of toys and "things" that money could buy, but what they really desired was for their parents to spend time with them. Children love for a grown-up to sit down and read them a story, play a game or just listen as they tell you all about things their little minds are thinking of. Take them for a walk, play ball, go fishing, bake cookies, camp out in the back yard. For years afterward, these are the memories that will be precious to them – not ones of sitting alone playing video games.

2) The gift of LOVE – We may just take for granted that we love our children and think they should know that. However, it is very important that we are demonstrating this love to them in many

ways. The most obvious is affection. Give them plenty of hugs, kisses and smiles each day. Bake them some cookies "just because". Give them encouragement and help when they need it. Write them some encouraging notes and slip them in their lunch box or on their pillow. Don't just know that you love them, show it to them.

3) The gift of DISCIPLINE – Yes, you read that right. Discipline, when administered with love, is a gift. It truly is doing your children a disservice to not correct and discipline when they need it. You are only reinforcing their lack of respect for your authority which will later translate to lack of respect for any authority (teachers, police officers, even God Himself). You also are teaching them that they don't experience any consequences for their behavior. And for the record, discipline is **not** waiting until all patience has been exhausted and you finally explode at them by screaming or even hitting them. Discipline with love is done immediately after they disobey and while you are still calm. Use the scriptures to show them why what they did was wrong. For example, if they tell a lie, read pertinent scriptures that deal with the sin of lying. The purpose of true discipline is to get to the heart of the matter rather than just take care of the surface behavior. The Bible gives several scriptures advocating discipline and how it is to be administered: Proverbs 10:13, Proverbs 22:15, Proverbs 23:13-14, Proverbs 19:18, Hebrews 12:8-10. The Bible itself does not suggest discipline as if it were an option. The Lord Himself administers discipline to us. Hebrews

12:6 tells us, *"For whom the Lord loves He chastens..."*

4) The gift of BRINGING UP YOUR CHILDREN IN THE LORD – Notice that I didn't say "the gift of taking your children to church". There is a huge difference in taking your kids to church and bringing them up in the Lord. If you are not teaching them to love the Lord supremely above all else and to develop a strong faith of their own in Him, you will most likely see them fall away as soon as they are grown if not sooner. Teaching them these things is a gift that should be bestowed upon them by their parents. While the preacher, elders and Bible class teachers play an important part in your child's spiritual education, it is the responsibility of the parents to make sure their child is given spiritual training. There are primarily two ways this is done: 1) Through direct teaching of the scriptures to your children and 2) Living a Christ-like example before them every day. First, you are to teach the scriptures to your children. Deuteronomy 6:7 instructs, *"you shall teach them diligently to your children, and shall talk of them when you sit in your house, when you walk by the way, when you lie down, and when you rise up."* This passage clearly teaches us that teaching our children the scriptures is a full-time daily job. Attending church services, while very important, will not be enough. Reading Bible stories to your children and then discussing them is a wonderful opportunity for all of you to learn together. Study both good and bad characters to learn what is good to do and not to

do. Spend time learning verses together to keep God's word in your hearts. Your children will need those verses to help them through temptations when you aren't there to guide them. Pray together, listing all of the things you are thankful for and being mindful of the needs of others. Play Bible trivia or games together. Second, live godly before them. It will do absolutely no good to teach them God's word daily if you won't live it yourself. Practice what you preach.

The gifts of time, love, discipline, and bringing them up in the Lord cannot be compared to anything that you can put under the Christmas tree. Love your children enough to give them the very best gifts of all.

****

What Will YOU Do?

There is a woman mentioned in the Bible in only six verses, but those six verses tell us a lot about the kind of woman she was. Her name was Dorcas and we read about her in Acts 9:36-41. We don't read about anything that she said, but plenty is said about what she did. She had gotten very sick and died when the apostle Peter was sent for. When he arrived at her house, there were widows who stood weeping, showing him the tunics and garments that Dorcas had made for them. Through the power of Jesus Christ, Peter raised her from the dead and presented her to the church and all of her friends who loved her so.

What can we learn from this short account of Dorcas' life? One of the things we learn about her was that she obviously had a talent that she could use to glorify the Lord and help those in need and she used it. Verse 36 tells us that she was a woman *"full of good works and charitable deeds which she did"*. The specific talent that is mentioned is sewing. She had made tunics and garments for the widows. Another thing we notice about her was that she saw a need and she filled it. There are so many opportunities to serve all around us if we will just open our eyes and hearts to them. Don't wait to be asked; be proactive! And finally, her death was clearly a loss to her community around her. She had made a noticeable difference. How are you making an impact in the lives of others?

God has given all of us talents that we can use for His glory and in His service. We need to make sure that we are using them. Now some have said, "There is nothing I can do." "I don't have any talents." "I don't have transportation, money, etc. to do anything." "I don't know *what* to do." Do you have a telephone? You can make calls to encourage, pray for and comfort people. Can you write? Write cards or letters. There are a lot of lonely, sad, and sick people who would love to receive a note in the mail. And don't forget about our service members serving far away from their family and friends. Can't afford to buy cards? Make them! My late grandmother was known for her card ministry. For over twenty years, she made cards using construction paper, copy paper, index cards or whatever she had. She decorated them with stickers or glitter and wrote little poems and scriptures inside. She couldn't drive a car, but she used a talent she did have to serve. Maybe you're a wonderful cook or baker. Why not bless someone with your efforts? Maybe you're an excellent gardener and can share your bounty with others who don't get much nutritious food. Maybe you can use your car to transport people to church, the doctor, or the store. Maybe you're like sister Dorcas and can sew or mend. Even just offering free babysitting to a single Mom or a busy set of parents can be a blessing.

Whatever it is, do something. God gives each and every one of us talents and opportunities to serve Him. We need to use them while we still have the time to do so. Each day is fresh with new opportunities. Read the story of Dorcas, make a list of things you can do to serve, then endeavor to do them. Follow her example and impact the lives of others around you for good.

****

"Therefore, as we have opportunity, let us do good to all, especially to those who are of the household of faith." ~Galatians 6:10

What Can I Do?

If you are too weak to journey up the mountain, steep and high,

You can stand within the valley while the multitudes go by.

You can chant in happy measure as they slowly pass along;

Though they may forget the singer, they will not forget the song.

If you have not gold or silver ever ready to command,

If you cannot toward the needy reach an ever-open hand,

You can visit the afflicted, o'er the erring you can weep;

You can be a true disciple, sitting at your Savior's feet.

Do not, then, stand idly watching for some greater work to do.

Go and toil in His vineyard, do not fear to do or dare;

If you want a field of labor you can find it anywhere.

What Is God's Purpose For Your Life?

When you were a little girl, what did you dream your life would be like? Did you picture yourself growing up to be a teacher or a ballerina? Did you see yourself as a mommy with little ones to play with and take care of? Or were you the hopeless romantic that dreamed you were a princess and one day your Prince Charming would come and carry you away? It's funny how we picture and plan our lives and they don't always quite turn out the way we thought. For one young lady, she never could have imagined in her wildest dreams what her life would be like. She never could have imagined she'd win a national beauty contest, become queen of a foreign empire, have her people (and herself) threatened with annihilation, be the person her people looked to to be an advocate to the king, and take her own life in her hands in order to spare her people. But this is exactly the purpose God had for the life of Esther.

Esther was an orphaned Jew under the care of her cousin, Mordecai. They lived in Persia as Jewish exiles when that nation conquered Babylon. We can read all about Esther's life in the book that bears her name in the Old Testament. The book is significant in that it is the only one in the Bible that doesn't mention God by name, yet it is filled with His presence, providence, and protection. It tells the story of the threat of annihilation to the Jews in Persia and their subsequent triumph as well as the part a young, beautiful Jewish orphan girl plays in her people's salvation.

How do we fulfill God's purpose for our life? Let's examine how Esther fulfilled hers:

1. She accepted the challenge to fit into God's plan. When the annihilation of the Jews is threatening, her cousin, Mordecai, pleads with her to use her influence with the king. Chapter 4, verse 14 is the key verse of the whole book. Mordecai asks her, *"For if you remain completely silent at this time, relief and deliverance will arise for the Jews from another place, but you and your father's house will perish. Yet who knows whether you have come to the kingdom for such a time as this?"* She never dreamed she would be chosen to be the queen of Persia and be in a position of power and influence, but she was and she accepted the responsibility placed on her to use her position to save her people.

2. She used what God had given her. Chapter 2, verse 7 tells us that she was lovely and beautiful and verses 9, 15 & 17 indicate she had a lovely character as well as she found favor with those put in charge of her and with the king himself. Her inner and outer beauty served her in being chosen as the queen of the Persian empire.

3. She remembered her position and stayed humble. After she was chosen queen and the royal crown was placed on her head, we read in chapter 2, verse 20 that, *"Esther had not yet revealed her kindred and her people, just as Mordecai had charged her, for Esther obeyed the command of Mordecai as when she was brought up by him."* She is a queen of Persia, and yet she remembers who she really is, a humble Jewish orphan. She still honors and respects the man who has brought her up and

cared for her by her obedience to him.

4. She had a sense of duty. Mordecai's words ring in her ears, "who knows whether you have come to the kingdom for such a time as this?" She knows she's not a queen just so she can play dress-up and make-believe. She is in this position for a reason of God's choosing. She has a duty to do all that she can to save her people and she acts accordingly. James 4:17 reminds us, *"Therefore, to him who knows to do good and does not do it, to him it is sin."*

Esther is a type of Christ. She was willing to sacrifice herself for her people and she was an advocate before the King on behalf of the Jews as Christ is an advocate on our behalf before the Father in heaven. Her rise from humble origins to queen of a mighty empire is a fascinating and exciting story, but we must always see the hand of God in it as He had a purpose for all that happened to her and for the position He placed her in.

If you know the end of the story, you will know that God does spare the Jews and they triumph over those who wanted to do them evil. God's people were spared and Esther played a huge part in their deliverance. God was glorified in the unlikely victory and the Jews commemorated the event every year with the Feast of Purim.

Every opportunity God gives us is one to bring honor and glory to His name. Ephesians 2:10 tells us, *"For we are His workmanship, created in Christ Jesus for good works, which God prepared beforehand that we should walk in them."* And I Peter 4:11 says, *"If anyone speaks, let him speak as the oracles of God. If anyone ministers, let him do it as with the ability which God supplies, that in all things God may be glorified through Jesus Christ, to whom belong the glory and the dominion forever and ever. Amen."*

What is God's purpose for *your* life? What does God expect *you* to do in such a time as this?

****

Heart to Heart: Devotional Thoughts for Women

Practical Application

The Northside Keepers at Home Girls Club has a handbook that lists requirements in order to earn badges for various skills. The most involved and challenging badge to earn is one called the "Proverbs 31 Study for Girls". The first requirement is to memorize Proverbs 31:10-31, the passage about the virtuous woman. Then all of the rest of the requirements break down this passage and require the girls to apply the individual verses in practical ways. For example, "*she...provides food for her household*" (v. 15) is followed by the requirement to cook several meals for her family. "*She...does not eat the bread of idleness*" (v. 27) is followed by the requirement to list ways she can do things each day to help her family and then practice doing them for a specified amount of time. They also have to make something for their family (economy), sew a dress for themselves, a garment for someone else in their family, plus many other things. The whole point of this badge is to teach them the biblical model of a woman who loves and serves God and her family and then to encourage these girls to *put into practice* what they are learning from these verses. It is a wonderful thing for these girls to memorize Proverbs 31, but how much more beneficial it is to them to do those things that are taught in the scriptures. It really doesn't do me much good to read about a woman who "*looks well to the ways of her household*", but yet let my family fend for themselves while I do what I want. I'm not applying the scripture "*she opens her mouth with wisdom and on her tongue is the law of kindness*" to my life if my speech is thoughtless and unkind to others. When I read "*she extends her hand to the poor, yes, she reaches out her hands to the needy", but won't show mercy or compassion to others, I am ignoring God's word.

James 1:22 says, *"But be doers of the word, and not hearers only, deceiving yourselves."* It is simply not enough to read the word of God and know what it says; we must also live it. James continues, *"For if anyone is a hearer of the word and not a doer, he is like a man observing his natural face in a mirror; for he observes himself, goes away, and immediately forgets what kind of man he was."*

I hope the girls in our club learn the valuable lesson of applying the scriptures to their lives and that they will see how important it is to be doers and not hearers only. I also hope that this encourages you to examine Proverbs 31 more closely and see if *you* can be described as a virtuous woman. If not, I encourage you to put those scriptures into practice in your life today. Don't just know it – live it!

****

"This Book of the Law shall not depart from your mouth, but you shall meditate in it day and night that you may be careful to do according to all that is written in it. For then you will make your way prosperous and then you will have good success."

~Joshua 1:8

****

The Proverbs 31 Woman

"Who can find a virtuous wife? For her worth is far above rubies. The heart of her husband safely trusts her; so he will have no lack of gain. She does him good and not evil all the days of her life. She seeks wool and flax and willingly works with her hands. She is like the merchant ships, she brings her food from afar. She also rises while it is yet night, and provides food for her household, and a portion for her maidservants. She considers a field and buys it; from her profits she plants a vineyard. She girds herself with strength, and strengthens her arms. She perceives that her merchandise is good, and her lamp does not go out by night. She stretches out her hands to the distaff, and her hand holds the spindle. She extends her hand to the poor. Yes, she reaches out her hands to the needy. She is not afraid of snow for her household, for all her household is clothed with scarlet. She makes tapestry for herself; her clothing is fine linen and purple. Her husband is known in the gates, when he sits among the elders of the land. She makes fine linen garments and sells them, and supplies sashes for the merchants. Strength and honor are her clothing; she shall rejoice in time to come. She opens her mouth with wisdom, and on her tongue is the law of kindness. She watches over the ways of her household and does not eat the bread of idleness. Her children rise up and call her blessed; her husband also, and he praises her. Many daughters have done well, but you excel them all. Charm is deceitful and beauty is vain, but a woman who fears the Lord, she shall be praised. Give her of the fruit of her hands, and let her own works praise her in the gates."

~Proverbs 31:10-31

The Role Of Women

Let's examine the scriptures to see God's plan for the role of women.

1. Position in relation to man:

    *Created from man – Gen. 2:22, *"Then the rib which the Lord God had taken from man He made into a woman, and He brought her to the man."*

    *Made to help man – Gen. 2:18, *"And the Lord God said, "It is not good that man should be alone; I will make him a helper comparable to him."*

    *Glory of man - I Cor. 11:7-9, *"For a man indeed ought not to cover his head, since he is the image and glory of God; but woman is the glory of man. For man is not from woman, but woman from man. Nor was man created for the woman, but woman for the man."*

    *Subject to man – Gen. 3:16, *"To the woman He said, 'I will greatly multiply your sorrow and your conception; in pain you shall bring forth children; your desire shall be for your husband, and he shall rule over you.'"*

    *Weaker than man - 1 Peter 3:7, *"Likewise you husbands, dwell with them with understanding, giving honor to the wife, as to the weaker vessel, and as being heirs together of the grace of life, that your prayers may not be hindered."*

2. Prohibitions not to:

    *Wear men's clothing – Deuteronomy 22:5, *"A

woman shall not wear anything that pertains to a man, nor shall a man put on a woman's garment, for all who do so are an abomination to the Lord your God."

*Have head shaved - I Cor. 11:6, *"For if a woman is not covered, let her also be shorn. But if it is shameful for a woman to be shorn or shaved, let her be covered."*

*Usurp authority - I Timothy 2:11, 12, *"Let a woman learn in silence with all submission. And I do not permit a woman to teach or to have authority over a man, but to be in silence."*

I Cor. 14:34, 35, *"Let your women keep silent in the churches, for they are not permitted to speak; but they are to be submissive, as the law also says. And if they want to learn something, let them ask their own husbands at home; for it is shameful for women to speak in church."*

3. Prompted to:

*Be submissive - I Peter 3:1, 2, *"Likewise you wives, be submissive to your own husbands, that even if some do not obey the word, they, without a word, may be won by the conduct of their wives, when they observe your chaste conduct accompanied by fear."*

*Be modest - I Timothy 2:9, 10, *"In like manner also, that the women adorn themselves in modest apparel, with propriety and moderation, not with braided hair or gold or pearls or costly clothing, but, which is proper for women professing godliness, with good works."*

*Have a gentle and quiet spirit - I Peter 3:3, 4, *"do not let your beauty be that outward adorning of arranging the hair, of wearing gold, or of putting on fine apparel; but let it be the hidden person of the heart, with the incorruptible ornament of a gentle and quiet spirit, which is very precious in the sight of God."*

*Love husband & children – Titus 2:4, *"That they admonish the young women to love their husbands, to love their children."*

*Be keepers at home – Titus 2:5, *"To be discreet, chaste, keepers at home, good, obedient to their own husbands, that the word of God may not be blasphemed."*

****

A Servant Of The Lord

A simple yet powerful statement is uttered in Luke 1:38 by Mary, the mother of Jesus. It is spoken after she has been told by the angel, Gabriel, that she will have a son – the Savior of the world! Mary responded, *"Behold, I am the servant of the Lord; let it be to me according to your word."*

What does it mean to be a servant of the Lord? The word Mary actually used is translated from the Greek word *doulos* meaning "bondservant" or "slave". Mary was indicating that she was not performing some casual service for the Lord, or serving Him when and if she felt like it or when it was convenient or appealing to her. Rather, Mary's choice of word indicated she was dedicating all of herself to the Lord; that His will would always trump her own and be carried out faithfully.

God calls us throughout the scriptures to be servants of His. Deuteronomy 10:12 states, *"...what does the Lord require of you, but to fear the Lord your God, to walk in all His ways, to love Him, to serve the Lord your God with all your heart and with all your soul".* Joshua issued this challenge which resounds today in chapter 24:15, *"choose this day whom you will serve...but as for me and my house, we will serve the Lord".* Jesus informs Satan in Matthew 4:10, *"...It is written, You shall worship the Lord your God and Him only shall you serve".* And the apostle Paul appeals to the Roman brethren in Romans 12:11, *"Do not be slothful in zeal, be fervent in spirit, serve the Lord".*

In so serving God, we are also called to serve others. Galatians 5:13 states, *"...through love serve one* another". I Peter 4:8-10 tells us that, *"Above all, keep loving one another earnestly, since love covers a multitude of sins. Show hospitality to one another without grumbling. As each has received a gift, use it to serve one another, as good stewards of God's grace"*.

Mary's statement reflects a heart dedicated to the Lord, a willing attitude and love for Him that rose above her own wants, needs, and even fears. What faith she displayed and what a fine example of godly womanhood she is to us today.

May each one of us exemplify that same faith and dedication to our Lord and boldly say like Mary, "I am the servant of the Lord."

****

S eek first things first.

E ndeavor to choose the good things.

R egard everything you do as for the Lord.

V iew life as a one-time opportunity.

E ngage in good works with all your heart.

****

God's Family

I sat quietly in the pew as the funeral was about to start. The church was full of mourners for one of our beloved members who had passed away. Sitting with me were some dear sisters in Christ. I remember feeling peaceful and comforted as I thought about how we were sitting and sharing our grief together as a family – God's family.

"Two are better than one, because they have a good reward for their toil. For if they fall, one will lift up his companion. But woe to him who is alone when he falls, and has not another to lift him up!" (Ecclesiastes 4:9, 10) King Solomon, the wisest man who ever lived, wrote these words thousands of years ago, yet how relevant they still are today.

We need each other. Plain and simple. God created us to be social beings, not isolated individuals. That is one of the reasons that God designed the church as it is. He knew how important it would be to an individual Christian's faith to worship with, fellowship with, and work with those of the same mind and faith. The early church took advantage of these blessings. Acts 2:46 tells us, *"And day by day, attending the temple together and breaking bread in their homes, they received their food with glad and generous hearts"*. They worshiped, worked, and fellowshiped together daily. It wasn't enough for them to see their brothers and sisters in Christ just once a week. They desired the fellowship on a daily basis. I'm sure since the church was just getting started and so many were just beginning their Christian walk, it was vitally important to receive strength and encouragement from people who were of like mind and faith. It was also the case that as many of them became Christians, their physical families disowned them. The church became their family. Many today have no one who cares anything about them or they have no one at all. How much they need to be in God's family as well!

We need to be with our fellow Christians to receive strength and encouragement as we struggle with the difficulties and sorrows of this life and as we journey together toward the same goal. The church is a family of brothers and sisters in Christ who love us as we are, who will, *"weep with those who weep and rejoice with those who rejoice"* (Romans 12:15). We are to be used as instruments in the hands of God to convey His love and comfort to others.

Many of our Northside members have lost a loved one within the last couple of years. What a great blessedness and comfort it has been for all of them to receive such an outpouring of love and support from the church. By the same token, we make announcements about the good events in people's lives so the church may rejoice with them and share in their happiness. What affects one member should be felt by the family collectively. I have experienced both sides of the coin, and in every case, I had the wonderful love and support of my church family. I was able to tangibly feel God's compassionate love for me through His church – my spiritual family. How sad it is when some come to the church only to sit alone and leave quickly, not wishing to be part of the whole. How much they miss! They miss work days and fall festivals, prayer breakfasts and potlucks, teachers meetings and Bible studies, decorating classrooms for Vacation Bible School and visiting the nursing home. They also miss someone to cry with when they're hurting, hugs from a dear sister in Christ, cards from people who care, prayers from those who love them, and the shared laughter of good friends.

Don't miss out on being a part of the greatest family there is – God's family.

****

God's Family

We're part of the family that's been born again;
Part of the family whose love knows no end;
For Jesus has saved us, and made us His own,
Now we're part of the family that's on its way home.

And sometimes we laugh together, sometimes we cry;
Sometimes we share together, heartaches and sighs;
Sometimes we dream together of how it will be
When we all get to heaven, God's family.

~Lanny Wolfe

****

A Servant Of The Church, Helper Of Many

In the book of Romans, the apostle Paul begins the final chapter with these words, *"I commend to you Phoebe our sister, who is a servant of the church in Cenchrea, that you may receive her in the Lord in a manner worthy of the saints, and assist her in whatever business she has need of you; for indeed she has been a helper of many and of myself also."* (Romans 16:1-2, NKJV)

Phoebe is a lesser-known character in the Bible as these two verses are the only mention of her, yet they tell us much about this remarkable Christian woman and her servant's heart.

Phoebe was a Christian who worshiped and worked with the congregation in Cenchrea. Cenchrea was a seaport about six miles east of Corinth where Paul was residing when he wrote his letter to the Romans. Paul gives quite a complimentary description of Phoebe as he refers to her as *"a servant of the church"* and *"a helper of many"*. The Greek word used for servant is *diakonon* from which we get our English word "deacon". In Acts 6, seven men were chosen to serve the widows in the church by seeing they received their portion of the daily distribution of food. These men were servants of the church and we commonly refer to them as the first seven deacons. Phoebe demonstrated this same type of service as being one was who was willing and able to assist others through her acts of charity and hospitality. She reminds me of Dorcas in Acts 9 as one who stayed busy utilizing her talents in service to the Lord.

It is thought that Phoebe might have been a woman

of means as she seemed to help others from her own resources, including the apostle Paul himself. In light of this, we can also see the characteristic of humility in Phoebe as she generously gave of her time and means, ministering in the humble role of a servant. She didn't do these good works in order that Paul would write a glowing report about her to others, she simply responded to the needs around her with the energy, enthusiasm and diligence that would please her Lord.

If you are ever at a loss as to what you can do to serve, just follow the example of Phoebe. Look around and see what needs to be done. Can you help prepare the communion trays? Can you wash dishes? Can you cook a meal? Can you encourage others through your words? Can you teach? Can you grade Bible correspondence lessons? Can you pray for missionaries? Can you use your own resources like Phoebe did to help support a missionary or assist a widow or to extend hospitality to a stranger? Service is not only for those that we know personally or like; it is an opportunity to do good to *all*. Galatians 6:10 tells us, *"Therefore, as we have opportunity, let us do good to all, especially to those who are of the household of faith."* Which is exactly what Phoebe tried to do.

Phoebe serves as a great role model and inspiration to us. Could it be said of you that you are a servant of the church and a helper of many? There is always something that each of us can do; let's get busy in service to our awesome God.

****

"For he who serves Christ in these things is acceptable to God and approved by men. Therefore let

us pursue the things which make for peace and the things by which one may edify another." ~Romans 14:18-19

****

The Christian Woman's Survival Kit

TOOTHPICK - to remind you to pick out the good qualities in others – Matthew 7:1

RUBBER BAND – to remind you to be flexible, things may not always go the way you want, but it will work out – Romans 8:28

BAND AID – to remind you to heal hurt feelings, yours or someone else's – Colossians 3:12-14

PENCIL – to remind you to list your blessings every day – Ephesians 1:3

ERASER – to remind you that everyone makes mistakes – Genesis 50:15-21

CHEWING GUM – to remind you to stick with it and you can accomplish anything – Philippians 4:13

MINT – to remind you that you are worth a mint to your heavenly Father – John 3:16

CANDY KISS – to remind you that everyone needs a hug or kiss - I John 4:7

TEA BAG – to remind you to relax daily and go over that list of God's blessings - I Thessalonians 5:18

****

Encouragement

Yes, I Can

As I was growing up, my father had these little "gems of wisdom" that he frequently passed on to us children. If repetition is the key to learning, then we should be well-educated! One of the gems my father often repeated was, "Can't died in the poorhouse!" He said this to us every time we whined, "I can't!" His point was that "can't" equates with "won't" and that effort must be put forth if we are to accomplish anything at all.

Now that I am a parent, I understand my father's frustration over hearing a child whine, "I can't!" This occurred in my home recently as my oldest son and I were working on a model of a medieval times city by the sea. It was tedious, time-consuming, and not something that could just be slapped together. My son's patience was gone within the first five minutes of working and the whining started. I told him that he could do it, it just required effort and patience.

I think the same applies to most everything else as well. The things we say we "*can't*" do are oftentimes things we most certainly *can* do if we would put forth the appropriate effort, cultivate patience to see it through, and pray for the strength and help that the Lord can provide.

Consider how different the lives of the following Bible characters would have been if they had said, "I can't":

- Would David have killed Goliath?
- Would Abraham have gone to the land of Moriah to sacrifice Isaac?
- Would Noah have built the ark?

- Would Solomon have built the temple?
- Would Moses have led the Israelites out of Egypt?
- Would the apostle Paul have continued to preach knowing the persecutions he would suffer?

Consider how different all of our lives would be if Jesus had decided He just couldn't die on the cross for all of mankind. None of these Bible characters used any supernatural ability to endure or persevere or accept the circumstances in their lives. They accomplished great things because they depended on the Lord to see them through.

Have you ever made any of these statements?...

- I can't deal with these kids.
- I can't quit smoking.
- I can't make this marriage work.
- I can't be a submissive woman in today's society.
- I can't give up alcohol altogether.
- I can't go to church every time the doors are opened.
- I can't teach a Bible class.
- I can't find the time for personal Bible study.
- I can't tell my friends about Jesus.
- I can't be a Christian.

I confess that I have made some of these statements myself. It doesn't take much effort to say, "I can't" and quit before you start. Truth be told, every time I responded with "I can't", I really meant, "I don't want to". Raising kids, having a great marriage, kicking a bad habit, working hard in the church, and even just being a Christian are things that take much time and effort. They are not just "slapped together" in five minutes any more than my son's model city was.

Whenever my children tell me, "I can't", they have to write or recite to me ten times, "*I **can** do all things through Christ which strengthens me*". (Philippians 4:13) As adults, we would do well to apply this to ourselves every time we are tempted to dig in our feet and declare that we just can't do something. Through Christ, we can. He says we can.

Type this verse and hang it up where you can read it every day. Memorize it and recite it to yourself. Negativity destroys and prevents great things. A positive attitude combined with the help of the Lord makes the impossible, possible. Whatever doubts are in your mind, whatever obstacles are in your way, whatever discouragement you face - overcome it all. Say, "Yes, I can!" and with Christ's help, you will!

****

Be Still And Know That I Am God

As I went into my oldest son's room one morning to awaken him for school, I loudly quoted Ephesians 5:14 which says, "...*Awake, you who sleep, arise from the dead, and Christ will give you light*". He rolled over and sleepily said, "Whatever happened to, 'Be still and know that I am God'?" (Psalm 46:10) I laughed at his witty response at the time, but thought more seriously about it later on. How often *are* we still enough to know our Lord? We live in such a fast-paced society with so many obligations and demands on our time, not to mention all of the opportunities for recreation and entertainment in our free time if we have any. How do we find the time to be calm and quiet so we may know God?

The first thing that the psalmist instructs us to do in this verse is to be still. We have a hard time communing with our Father in heaven when we are constantly running around. We have to take the time, **make the time**, to just sit and be still. (And this doesn't mean sitting still to watch TV or surf the internet!) The verse finishes by saying, "*and know that I am God*". We must use our time to be growing spiritually through prayer and personal worship to God and study and meditation of His Word. Only in taking time to do this daily will we find ourselves growing in the Lord and more willing and able to do His Will.

I have often found that even in my busiest of days, if I have made the time to be still long enough to pray to the Lord and study His word and worship Him *before* all of my activities for the day, I had a productive day and seemed to accomplish all I needed to do. Other busy days when I felt that there just wasn't time enough to "be still", often ended with frustration and stress. Starting our day out right by making time for the Lord will enable us to have the peace of mind to do what we must as we place ourselves in the capable hands of our Father. It also prepares us to live more righteously and holy for Him.

Let us be careful that we do not put God on the back burner until there is more time. Let us have a happier and more holy life in the midst of a world of chaos by taking the time to be still and know that He is God.

****

Time to Pray

I got up quite early one morning and rushed right into the day;

I had so much to accomplish I took no time to pray.

The problems just tumbled about me, and heavier came each task;

"Why doesn't God help me?", I wondered. He said, "Why didn't you ask?"

I saw naught of joy or beauty. The day sped on gray and bleak;

I asked, "Why won't the Lord show me?" He said, "But you didn't seek."

I tried to come into God's presence; I used all my keys at the lock,

God gently, lovingly chided, "My child, why didn't you knock?"

I woke up quite early one morning and paused upon entering the day;

There was so much to accomplish, I HAD to take time to pray.

~Author Unknown

****

Waiting

Don't you hate to wait? We're busy people and we certainly don't like to waste time waiting in traffic or in lines at the store or in the waiting room at the doctor's office. What about waiting for other things – like waiting for our finances to improve, waiting for our relationships with our spouse and children to get better, waiting for God to finally answer that prayer we've been praying in the way we want, waiting for our circumstances in life to just change. It's hard to wait, isn't it? Because the truth is, we don't always have a lot of patience.

Isaiah 40:31 says, *"They that wait upon the Lord shall renew their strength; they shall mount up with wings like eagles, they shall run and not grow weary, they shall walk and not faint."* Sometimes God is requiring us to wait on purpose. Maybe it is to strengthen our faith or to teach us a lesson we need to learn or maybe just to teach us some patience that we so badly need. Think about some of the great Bible characters who had to wait. Abraham and Sarah were promised a child after they had already grown old and past childbearing years, yet how long did they have to wait for the promise of God to be fulfilled? Abraham was 100 years old and Sarah was 90 when Isaac was born. That's a long time to trust in God to fulfill a promise, isn't it? Yet God kept His word and gave them the son of promise and filled their lives with such joy. And what about Joseph? He was wrongly enslaved and then imprisoned for years before his release and rise to the position of second in command of all of Egypt. Although he suffered for a season in his life, God was faithful and never forgot about him, but blessed him beyond what Joseph could have ever imagined. Mary and Martha had a sick brother, Lazarus, that they knew their friend Jesus could heal, and yet Jesus waited until Lazarus had been dead for four days before arriving. Mary and Martha suffered true grief, but were blessed with unspeakable joy when Jesus raised their brother from the dead. It had been his purpose to delay his coming in order to do this miracle.

So many times we don't understand why things happen in our lives. We struggle with wanting to know the future and we chafe with impatience as to when our circumstances will change. We must be careful that we do not fall into the trap that Satan sets for us so often. Satan is the father of lies (John 8:44) and he is feeding us lies about our lives. He works hard to plant seeds of doubt that will eventually grow to destroy our faith if we let them take root in our minds. Things such as, "I shouldn't have to suffer like this!" "This is going to go on forever; things will never get any better!" "I just can't take any more." "If my circumstances would just be different, I would be different." What does the truth of God's word say to counter these thoughts? James 1:2-4 says, *"My brethren, count it all joy when you fall into various trials, knowing that the testing of your faith produces patience. But let patience have its perfect work, that you may be complete, lacking nothing."* God intends for suffering to serve a purpose in our life that will strengthen us and make us complete if we will let it. We also must remember that Jesus himself was not immune to suffering in this world. II Corinthians 11:22-30 gives a description of the sufferings and trials of the apostle Paul, yet he never gave up. He never said, "I can't take any more." Why is that? Because he always kept his eyes on the goal –

being with the Lord in heaven. *"I press toward the goal for the prize of the upward call of God in Christ Jesus."* (Philippians 3:14) When we take our eyes off of our goal as a Christian and focus on the sorrows of this life, then we will be tempted to give up and give in. Lift your eyes to the Lord. (Psalm 121:1,2)

Finally, we need to realize and admit that our circumstances do not make us what we are; they merely reveal what we are already. If we cannot be happy in our present circumstance, we're not likely to be happy in any other either. We cannot let our circumstances control us. We *can* choose to have joy in our Lord despite whatever we're going through in this life.

Waiting is a deliberate action which requires learning contentment despite our circumstances, faith and trust in the Lord, and obedience to Him. If we will learn to keep our eyes on the goal like Paul, to have faith like Abraham and Sarah, to trust in the Lord like Joseph, and to be obedient by waiting on the Lord patiently, we will have true joy and peace in our lives and God will renew our strength and bless us more than we can imagine. Just wait and see!

****

Faith and Doubt

Doubt sees the obstacles; Faith sees the way.

Doubt sees the darkest night; Faith sees the day.

Doubt dreads to take a step; Faith soars on high.

Doubt questions, "Who believes?"; Faith answers, "I!"

****

A Lesson In Persistence

We have a bird feeder in our back yard. Our son, Matthew, loves birds and wanted to be able to observe them close-up so we placed a feeder on a metal shepherd's hook several feet outside our dining room window. Now we realize that squirrels love to eat bird seed so we thought we could be proactive in dealing with this problem. We placed the metal pole a few feet away from the trunk of a tree. Then we smeared Vaseline all up the pole of the plant hook so the squirrels couldn't climb up from the ground. We sat back smugly to enjoy the birds over the next few days without the interference of squirrels. It took a few days for word to get out, but the squirrels finally started converging on the site to do reconnaissance. They would stand on the ground at the base of the pole and look upward, longingly at the feeder. They didn't make any attempts to go up the pole – at first. But after a few days, one of them jumped on the pole and scrambled upward, only to slide down like a fireman on a pole. We laughed as we watched his fruitless attempts. After a few more tries, the squirrel gave up climbing the pole. We thought, "Aha!" "We have gotten the better of the squirrel population in this neighborhood!" They were not, however, to be so easily outdone. We then started noticing them climbing the tree trunk and jumping onto the metal hook that our hummingbird feeder was on. (Right next to the hook with the seed feeder.) At first, their weight made the hook sway so that they would jump down immediately. But they kept trying and soon got over the fear of the swaying hook. Eventually, success! Imagine our surprise when we saw a squirrel hanging upside down on our feeder, eating to his heart's content. Once they discovered the way to the object of their desire, there was no stopping them. They cleaned us out in a day. We moved the hook further away from the tree to prevent jumping and once more smeared Vaseline up the pole. Within an hour, one curious squirrel was already on the ground at the base of the pole, looking up and I am sure the wheels of his little mind were already turning. Needless to say, we are still fighting an ongoing battle with the squirrels to keep them out of the bird feeder.

Now, the point is this: the squirrels had a goal – the bird feeder, and they kept their eyes on that goal and NOTHING deterred them from reaching it. They worked day after day and hour after hour until they finally had success. No obstacle was too great for them to overcome. No challenge was too daunting.

Our goal is heaven. We should have our eyes fixed on it at all times and should let NOTHING deter us from reaching it. We should be diligently working to reach our goal day after day and hour after hour. There is no obstacle too great for us to overcome, no challenge is too daunting.

There are enough squirrels in Pinellas County to be a daily reminder of persistence. Next time you see one, think about how determined they are to reach their goals in life and then think about how determined you are to reach yours at the end of this life. Persist until you reach it!

****

"And let us not grow weary while doing good, for in due season we shall reap if we do not lose heart."

~Galatians 6:9

****

Be A Barnabas

What is something that from time to time everyone needs, doesn't cost a cent, and most everyone has the ability to give? Encouragement! Encouragement may be defined as "being heartened, something that cheers and helps on". Of course, the opposite of encouragement is discouragement. Since the beginning of time, Satan has used this powerful tool to cripple and weaken God's people. This tool of Satan is so effective that he still uses it today, but we can combat this tool with one of our own – encouragement.

Barnabas is a man we read about in the New Testament, but is not someone we usually consider to be a "major" Bible character. Generally when we think of him we say, "Oh, yeah, he's the guy that went on some missionary journeys with Paul", but there's a lot more to him than that!

His name, Barnabas, means "son of encouragement". He was one of many Christians who sold his land and gave the money to the apostles for those Christians who were in need (Acts 4:36, 37). He stood up for the apostle Paul when the disciples at Jerusalem were fearful of him (Acts 9:27). But one of the best passages of scripture which sums up his life is found in Acts 11:23-24 which says, "*When he came and had seen the grace of God, he was glad, and* **encouraged them all** *that with purpose of heart they should continue with the Lord. For he was a good man, full of the Holy Spirit and of faith.*" From his name down to his words and deeds, Barnabas was an encourager.

Could the same be said of us? Have you told a Bible class teacher they were doing a great job lately? Are you watching for that weak brother or sister who is so easily discouraged in their walk with the Lord? What about a shut-in or someone dealing with a serious illness who could use some sunshine in their lives? When was the last time you encouraged your preacher in his never-ending work?

Being an encourager is such an important job, is so needed, and so appreciated. We've all fallen prey to Satan's tool of discouragement at one time or another. What a blessing it is, then, when someone comes along and says encouraging words or does something to boost our spirits. It's like a breath of fresh air! Resolve to do all that you can to fight the tool of discouragement and bring encouragement to the lives of others – be a Barnabas!

****

Spring Cleaning

Spring is in the air and new life is beginning all around us. The trees are budding, flowers are blooming, baby animals are being born. Something about springtime just feels fresh and new after the somewhat dreariness of the end of winter when the grass, trees, and flowers are dead. This time of year gets me in the mood to do some revamping in my house and getting around to fixing and freshening things up. I do the inside of my house and the outside as well. This past weekend I raked the old, dead leaves out of the flowerbed, weeded it, planted new flowers and laid new mulch. Then I washed windows and the front of the house, cleaning away accumulated dirt and grime. Now the outside of the house is looking better, and that is what most people see as they drive by. But wouldn't it seem kind of odd to have a beautiful yard, flower bed and spotless house outside and then have the inside filthy? The inside of the house should be cleaned up and look as nice as the outside.

Not everybody sees what you look like on the inside. Maybe you hide it really well by showing them a beautiful exterior, but the Lord sees what you are like on the inside and nothing can be hidden from Him. He sees everything that is in your heart whether it be clean and pure, or dirty and sinful. (I Samuel 6:7)

Now if I don't get all of my "sprucing up" done in the spring, I can certainly do yardwork and clean up my house in the summer. There is no specific window of time that I am allotted to clean up. If you need to do some cleaning in your heart, it's never too late. There is no better time than right now to do some serious self-examination and make changes that you know need to be made. David said in Psalm 51:10, "*Create in me a clean heart, O God, and renew a steadfast spirit within me*".

With all of the new beginnings taking place in the world around you, what better time could there be for a new beginning in your walk with the Lord? Start your spiritual spring cleaning today!

****

Needing some help in doing a self-examination? Here's some questions for you to ask yourself in order to do a...

Spiritual Check-Up

1. Are the church services boring to me? _____
2. Have I missed some worship services in the last month? ___
3. Have I forgotten the last time I memorized a Bible verse? _____
4. Has my Bible sat unopened in my house all week long? _____
5. Have more than 24 hours gone by without offering a prayer to God? _____
6. Has it been several months since I have invited someone to church or shared the gospel with them? _____
7. Can I remember the last good deed I did for someone without expecting something in return? _____
8. Have I followed the scripture's plan for being a submissive Christian woman with a gentle and

quiet spirit? _____

9. Have I had a bitter, ugly, or negative attitude over things in my life rather than a heart full of thankfulness to God for the good things? _____

10. Have I forgotten what a precious gift I received when I was saved? _____

If you answered "yes" to any of these, then be assured you're human! However, let them serve as an indicator of areas of poor spiritual health that need to be treated and made vibrant and healthy again. *"Be strong in the Lord and in the power of His might."* (Ephesians 6:10)

****

Blessings In The Midst Of Suffering

"Does Jesus care when my heart is pained too deeply for mirth and song; as the burdens press, and the cares distress, and the way grows weary and long?

Does Jesus care when my way is dark with a nameless dread and fear? As the daylight fades into deep night shades, does He care enough to be near?

Does Jesus care when I've tried and failed to resist some temptation strong; when for my deep grief I find no relief; tho my tears flow all the night long?

Does Jesus care when I've said "goodbye" to the dearest on earth to me, and my sad heart aches till it nearly breaks – is it aught to Him? Does He see?"[1]

These are the touching and oh-so-true-to-life words of an old, beautiful hymn. Have you ever felt this way? Have you ever felt so sad and hurt so much that you felt your heart literally ache? Have you wondered why God allows you to suffer and to hurt both physically and emotionally? Believe it or not, there are blessings to be discovered in the midst of suffering.

Consider the following:

- Suffering is a part of our world and our lives because sin is in the world. Sin causes sorrow and suffering.
- Suffering gives us an opportunity to draw closer to our Father in heaven. Satan has no sympathy for us when we hurt, God does. I Peter 5:7 says, *"Casting all your care upon Him, for He careth for you."*
- Suffering helps us to empathize with and help

others who go through similar situations that we have experienced. Galatians 6:2 tells us to, "*Bear one another's burdens.*" and Romans 12:15 reminds us to, "*...weep with those who weep.*"

- Suffering should create in us a stronger desire and longing for heaven. If our life here on earth was painless and perfect, would we really desire to leave it for heaven? Amid our suffering, we can have the assurance that the day will come when we will have complete relief, rest, happiness, and peace – the day we go home to live forever with God our Father. If we had no hope of that in our future, we would be as the apostle Paul states in I Corinthians 15:19, "*most miserable.*"

- Suffering will not go on forever if we have salvation in Christ Jesus. Jeremiah 29:11 assures us, "*For I know the thoughts that I think toward you, says the Lord, thoughts of peace and not of evil, to give you a future and a hope.*" Our future, our hope rests in our Lord and Savior and the home in heaven with Him that we are promised.

The chorus of the hymn mentioned above comforts us with these words: "Oh yes, He cares; I know He cares, His heart is touched with my grief. When the days are weary, the long nights dreary, I <u>know</u> my Savior cares!"

[1] "Does Jesus Care" Frank E. Graeff, J. Lincoln Hall

****

Need help coping with suffering? Here's some suggestions to put into practice:

1. TALK – Whether it be your spouse, a family member, a trusted friend, or a church leader, find someone to confide in when you need to unload some of your feelings. If need be, write them down in a journal.

2. CRY – God gave us a built-in pressure release: tears, so don't be afraid to use it. A good cry can help you feel better physically afterward. It helps to release stress and tension that gets bottled up inside.

3. ACCEPT – Work on accepting the things that cannot be changed in your life. Ask the Lord for help with this.

4. REACH OUT – Find someone that you can help. This serves two purposes. First, it gives aid to someone who needs it. Second, it helps you take your mind off of your own troubles for a while.

5. STUDY – Turn to the comfort of the Scriptures. Spend time daily in God's Word. Read accounts of people who suffered and made it through (Job, Joseph, and Ruth just for starters). Read the beautiful descriptions of heaven.

6. PRAY – The most important thing you can do. Pour your whole heart out to the Lord. He's always there, always listening, and always caring.

****

"Let not your heart be troubled...I go to prepare a place for you." ~John 14:1-2

Time

"To everything there is a season and a time for every purpose under heaven..." (Ecclesiastes 3:1) This begins a familiar text in verses 1 through 8 about time; more specifically how there is a time for everything. Now as women, most of us are throwing up our hands and saying we don't have much time for **anything** much less **everything**. Maybe this article will be able to help a little.

Time is very precious because it is limited. No one is able to add another month to a year, week to a month, hour to a day, or even a second to a minute. The time we have in our mortal lives is limited. None of us can live forever. Because time is limited and precious, we need to be good stewards of it by doing the following:

1. **Prioritize** – In reading Matthew 6:25-34, we can see how God provides those things which we have need of in our lives. There are some who worry and fret and labor trying to make sure they have food and clothing, but it is a waste of their valuable time to worry so. The Lord assures us in v. 33 that all of these things will be taken care of (*"added to you"*) if we'll seek his kingdom **first**. One of the problems we have with managing our time wisely is that we're putting too many other things ahead of God in our life. The Lord tells us to put Him first and everything else will fall into place. He knows just what we have need of in our lives and is ready to give it to us if we will just let go of our worry and rushing around trying to handle everything ourselves. I think too often we find ourselves preoccupied

with "living life" and tend to stuff God into the little cracks of time we have leftover. If we happen to have our work done and have no errands to run at the time and of course we're not too worn out (does that *ever* happen?), then, yes, we'll attend a mid-week Bible study or work day at the church or make that visit to the hospital. We are only fooling ourselves if we think God is pleased with our leftovers. As Christians who love and serve Him with all of our hearts, the only natural response is that we will worship Him and do His will at every opportunity. Putting Him first will not make our life harder or more hectic; rather, it will bless and enhance our life to the fullest measure. Start each and every day with prayer. No, you are not too busy for that. If you must, pray in the shower, or in the car, or over breakfast. Humbly ask the Father to help you accomplish what you need to do that day and I guarantee that your days will be productive and more peaceful if you have the hand of almighty God guiding you through it. Just ask Him, He is there to help you. Continue putting Him first by reading and studying your Bible every day. This can be at breakfast, lunch, after dinner, before bed, whenever. It's amazing how much better you feel and how much more you get done when you truly put God first. Honestly answer this question: Do you find time for what you *want* to do? Maybe you have a favorite TV show that you never miss or you treat yourself to a spa day or shopping trip. Now I'm not knocking having leisure time to relax and refresh yourself. Jesus himself took time to get away and rest. The point is that we really do make time for what we want to do, don't we? Are we making time to do what we want and yet still not "finding" time to serve the Lord as we should? Think prayerfully about this. Getting our priorities right is a huge first step in becoming good stewards of our time.

2. **Prepare** – Being organized and efficient in our daily routine will go a long way in managing our time better. Sit down briefly on Saturday evening or Sunday afternoon and glance at your week. Making lists, noting appointments and planning errands and your things to do will help you better organize your time. More importantly than being prepared in our daily lives, we need to be constantly making preparations for eternity. Jesus tells us in John 9:4 that *"the night cometh when no man can work"*. On judgment day, all of our "important" errands and meetings and activities will not seem important at all anymore. It will be too late to squeeze in some preparation for eternity in at that point. We must prepare now while we have time and opportunity. This goes back to our first point of putting God first.

3. **Pray** - I read a bumper sticker the other day which said, "I am woman, I am invincible, I am tired!" You know, even though we try to do it all, we simply cannot. We are not invincible and we can't do it alone. Jeremiah 10:23 tells us, *"O, Lord, I know the way of man is not in himself; it is not in man that walketh to direct his own steps"*. James 1:5, 6 assures us that we can ask God for wisdom and guidance and it will be given to us. We truly need the wisdom of God to

make the best decisions in the use of our time each day. And perhaps most reassuring of all are the words we find in Philippians 4:13 which proclaim, *"I can do all things through Christ which strengthens me"*.

There is the secret to being the best stewards of our time that we can be: We CAN do all things by seeking God and His kingdom first, being prepared for here and for eternity, and praying for the wisdom and strength that only the Lord can give us. May God bless us all as we live our lives each day to serve Him.

****

Overcoming Discouragement: God's 3-step Process

In I Kings chapter 19, the prophet Elijah is facing some pretty heavy discouragement. He had just been through the showdown on Mt. Carmel against the prophets of Baal and now the king and queen of Israel want him dead so he is in hiding. He is physically and mentally exhausted and emotionally at the bottom of the barrel as he feels there is no one else in all Israel who serves the Lord but him. So he does what anyone else in his position would do: have a pity party. In verse 4 of this chapter he cries out to the Lord to just let him die, but God isn't finished with him yet. The Lord gives Elijah what he needs - a strong dose of encouragement in three steps.

First, the Lord recognizes Elijah's physical and mental tiredness and lets him have some much-needed rest. In verses 5-8, Elijah sleeps, then an angel prepares food for him, then he sleeps some more, then the angel prepares more food for him. Verse 8 says that he went on the strength of that food for the next forty days and night. (I want the recipe!) When we're discouraged, maybe we just need to step back from everything, take a break and rest up. Eating a proper, healthy diet and getting plenty of sleep does wonders for rejuvenating our bodies.

Next, the Lord reassures Elijah that he is not alone. In verse 10, Elijah complains to the Lord that he has been very zealous for him, but he is the only faithful one left and now there's a death threat against him. Yet, God corrects his misconception. In verse 18, the Lord lets Elijah know that there are 7,000 in Israel who have not turned to idolatry, but remain true to God. It's always mentally uplifting to realize we're not alone in whatever we're going through. Elijah now realizes that he does have people he can turn to for help and support.

Finally, God gives him work to do. In verses 15 & 16, the Lord sends him on a journey to go and anoint two kings and a prophet. Discouragement only sets in deeper the longer we sit and dwell on it. Diverting our mind with productive work goes a long way in dispelling gloomy thoughts.

If it worked for Elijah, it can work for us. Overcome discouragement God's way by resting, being reassured through the word of God and fellow Christians that you're not alone, and finding productive work to do in the Lord's kingdom.

****

"Have I not commanded you? Be strong and of good courage; do not be afraid, nor be dismayed, for the Lord your God is with you wherever you go."

~Joshua 1:9

****

Trust In The Lord

Do you consider yourself a control freak? I do. I like the feeling of being able to handle anything that comes my way and just about pull my hair out when there is something outside the realm of my control. The reality is that everything really is outside the realm of my control. It all lies in the hands of God.

One of the things I struggle with the most is learning to let go of worry and fear and to put my trust in my Father in heaven. Faith is a monumental kind of trust. It is not a trust that says, "I'll trust you when I see everything turn out all right," but one that says, "I'll trust you even though I don't know what the outcome will be." King Solomon realized the value of this kind of trust when he wrote the following words in the book of Proverbs: "*...whoever trusts in the Lord shall be safe.*" (Proverbs 29:25b) and "*...whoever trusts in the Lord, happy is he.*" (Proverbs 16:20b)

"*God has not given us a spirit of fear...*" (II Timothy 1:7). Worry and fear are heavy and unnecessary burdens we carry. Jesus said in regard to worry, "*Which of you by worrying can add one cubit to his stature?...Therefore, do not worry about tomorrow, for tomorrow will worry about its own things.*" (Matthew 6:27, 34) Worry and fear do nothing productive, but rather drain us of necessary energy to face the tasks at hand. They also weaken our faith and draw us farther away from the one true source of help and comfort.

When we are faced with the unknown and there is nothing we can do to control an outcome, we need to commit the situation, person, etc. to God's care and

Heart to Heart: Devotional Thoughts for Women

keeping. My oldest son is in the army and will deploy to Afghanistan sometime this year. As a mother it is easy to start worrying and getting upset about what might happen to him there, but as a Christian mother, I have committed him into the hands of my God and I know that there is no better place that he can be. It gives me a peace that surpasses all understanding when I place my trust in the Lord and not in myself or other people or circumstances over which I'm not in control. Paul writes some reassuring words in Philippians 4:6 & 7 when he says, *"Be anxious for nothing, but in everything by prayer and supplication with thanksgiving, let your requests be made known unto God and the peace of God which surpasses all understanding will guard your hearts and minds in Christ Jesus."*

God wants us to have peace in our hearts, to be free from the burdens of worry, fear, and anxiety and He gives us a way to do it. Read His words of love and comfort. Read His promises and let your faith be strengthened by them. Commit your cares to Him in prayer and live in calm reassurance that God is in control so that you can say like the Psalmist, *"O Lord of hosts, blessed is the man who trusts in You!"* (Psalms 84:12)

****

"Trust in the Lord with all thy heart and lean not on thine own understanding. In all thy ways acknowledge Him and He shall direct thy paths."

~Proverbs 3:5-6

****

Is Your Hut Burning?

You may have read the following article as it made the rounds on the internet several years ago. It is a powerful message of God's everlasting care and providence, protection, and plan for our lives. Just when you think all hope is gone and you've reached the bottom, God can raise you up and marvelous things can happen...

The only survivor of a shipwreck was washed up on a small, uninhabited island. He prayed feverishly for God to rescue him, and every day he scanned the horizon for help, but none seemed forthcoming. Exhausted, he eventually managed to build a little hut out of driftwood to protect him from the elements, and to store his few possessions.

But then one day, after scavenging for food, he arrived home to find his little hut in flames, the smoke rolling up to the sky. The worst had happened; everything was lost. He was stunned with grief and anger: "God, how could you do this to me!" he cried.

Early the next day, however, he was awakened by the sound of a ship that was approaching the island. It had come to rescue him. "How did you know I was here?" asked the weary man of his rescuers. "We saw your smoke signal," they replied.

It is easy to get discouraged when things are going bad, but we shouldn't lose heart because God is at work in our lives, even in the midst of pain and suffering. Remember, the next time your little hut is burning to the ground it just may be a smoke signal that summons the grace of God.

Author Unknown

What Are You Anchored To?

"Will your anchor hold in the storms of life, when the clouds unfold their wings of strife? When the strong tides lift, and the cables strain, will your anchor drift, or firm remain?"[1] These are some questions that are asked in a familiar hymn and I think they give us some food for thought.

Everyone is trying to anchor themselves to something or someone. No one likes to feel adrift, especially when the difficult days come and we face the "storms of life". We want something solid to cling to to help us survive. The problem is that what most people are clinging to is not at all secure and will only set them further adrift and ultimately cause them to perish.

Some people try to anchor themselves to money. They feel that if they could just have enough of it, they would be secure no matter what they face in life. I think we can see from history (for example, the stock market crash of 1929), that money is not the answer. It can be taken away or lost in a moment. It is something material that can never be possessed with any real sense of security.

Some people anchor themselves to a position. If they can just be in a position of power in their job, family, etc. then they feel they have a sense of control over things. But positions can change, authority can pass from one to another, and ultimately the control they believed they possessed is then gone.

Some people anchor themselves to a person. They put all their eggs in this one basket of a relationship only to find that people will let you down – even the ones you love the most.

Sadly, some anchor themselves to substances that destroy their minds and bodies because they think they can't cope with this world without them.

All of these things are flimsy anchors. They will not hold when "the strong tides lift and the cables strain". But wait! There is hope! The chorus of the hymn continues in this way, "We have an anchor that keeps the soul steadfast and sure while the billows roll, fastened to the Rock which cannot move, grounded firm and deep in the Savior's love." Praise the Lord for His steadfastness! We can anchor ourselves to the Rock which will never be moved and will always hold safely and securely no matter what comes our way.

David expressed the steadfastness of the Lord so many times in his writings. Psalm 16:8 says, *"I have set the Lord always before me; because He is at my right hand, I shall not be shaken."* Psalm 31:3 says, *"For You are my rock and my fortress; therefore, for Your name's sake, lead me and guide me."* Psalm 94:22 says, *"But the Lord has been my defense, and my God the rock of my refuge."* And, finally, one of my favorite passages, Psalm 18:1-3 says, *"I love you, O Lord, my strength. The Lord is my rock and my fortress and my deliverer, my God, my rock, in whom I take refuge, my shield, and the horn of my salvation, my stronghold. I call upon the Lord, who is worthy to be praised, and I am saved from my enemies."*

When you feel as if you're drifting in a huge sea of despair as the waves crash around you, these words from the holy scriptures can give you such comfort, peace and security. Nothing moves our Lord! We can cling to Him always and He will be our unmovable rock and shield and fortress.

So, what are you anchored to? Have you built for yourself a false sense of security by anchoring yourself to things that aren't lasting and strong? Fasten yourself to The Rock which cannot move and be grounded firm and deep in our Savior's wonderful love!

1 We Have An Anchor by Priscilla J. Owens

****

The Three "P's" Of Promise

Isaiah 43:1-3 is one of my favorite passages of scripture. It never fails to uplift and inspire me and to reassure me of God's love and care. There are 3 wonderful promises contained in this passage and to make them easy to remember, they all begin with "P". First, let's look at the verses themselves; listen closely as God speaks to your heart:

"...Fear not, for I have redeemed you; I have called you by your name; you are mine. When you pass through the waters, I will be with you; and through the rivers, they shall not overflow you. When you walk through the fire, you shall not be burned, nor shall the flame scorch you. For I am the Lord your God, The Holy One of Israel, your Savior."

The first promise we see is contained in the beginning of verse 2 – the promise of <u>His presence</u>. *"When you pass through the waters,* **I will be with you**.*"* What do you think the Israelites thought of when they read or heard these words? Would they think back in their history when God's mighty hand parted the Red Sea so they could cross on dry land and escape Pharaoh's army? Would their minds go forward a few decades to the time when Joshua began to lead them into the promised land and God parted the Jordan River? They would remember God's powerful presence in these instances and many others in their lives. Isn't it comforting to know that the same God is with us today even in situations that seem insurmountable to us? Hebrews 13:5b reassures us, *"For He himself has said, 'I will never leave you nor forsake you.'"*

The second promise is found in the middle of the

same verse – the promise of His peace. "*...and through the rivers, **they shall not overflow you**.*" Do you ever get so overwhelmed that you feel like you're drowning? That's not a very calm, peaceful feeling, is it? But, we can overcome whatever is pulling us down because God is more powerful than whatever threatens to engulf us. Psalm 29:3 says, "*The voice of the Lord is over the waters; the God of glory thunders; the Lord is over many waters.*" And in the same chapter, verse 11b, we read, "*...The Lord will bless His people with peace.*"

The third promise is found in the last part of verse 2 – the promise of His protection. "*When you walk through the fire, **you shall not be burned, nor shall the flame scorch you**.*" Every time I get to this part, I can't help but wonder if these very words in Isaiah were going through the minds of Shadrach, Meshach, and Abednego as they were being led to the fiery furnace. Their faith in the Lord and in His protection resulted in their coming out of the fire unscathed and without even the smell of smoke upon them. Our God is so awesome! Just think of how God's protection can envelope us as well. We truly have nothing to fear.

This passage of scripture began with God's gentle reassurance to, "*Fear not*" because we are His. He knows and cares about each one of us so specifically, "*I have called you by your name; you are mine.*" What wonderful promises have been given to God's people to give us all hope, comfort, and reassurance. The reason we can trust in these promises of His presence, His peace, and His protection is summed up at the end of this passage: "*For I am the Lord your God, the Holy One of Israel, your Savior.*"

****

Just For Fun

Heart to Heart: Devotional Thoughts for Women

Can You Figure This Out?

This puzzle was written by a lady in California in 1890 in response to a gentleman in Philadelphia who said he would pay $1,000 to anyone who could write a puzzle that he could not solve. He failed to do so and paid the lady $1,000 (a great sum at that time). The answer is one word, five letters long and appears 4 times in the KJV of the Bible. An eight year old boy figured this out. Can you?

"God made Adam out of the dust, but thought it best to make me first. So I was made according to God's holy plan. My whole body God made complete, without arms, or hands, or legs, or feet. My ways and acts did God control, but in my body He placed no soul. A living being I became, and Adam gave to me a name. Then from His presence I withdrew, for this man Adam I never knew. All my Maker's laws I do obey, and from these laws I never stray. Thousands of me go in fear, but seldom on the earth appear. Later, for a purpose God did see, He placed a living soul in me. But that soul of mine God had to claim, and from me took it back again. And when this soul from me had fled, I was the same as when first made; without arms, legs, feet, or soul, I travel on from pole to pole. My labors are from day to night, and to men I once furnished light. Thousands of people both young and old, did by my death bright lights behold. No right or wrong can I conceive; the Bible and it's teachings I can't believe. The fear of death doesn't trouble me; pure happiness I will never see. And up in heaven I can never go, nor in the grave or hell below. So get your Bible and read with care. You'll find my name recorded there."

Can You Find 20 Books Of The Bible In This Paragraph?

Someone showed me this story and remarked that there are twenty books of the Bible hidden here. He challenged me to find them. Sure enough they're all here. Still this thing's a lulu, kept me looking so hard for the longest time. Someone of you will get bogged down with facts, others are hit by them like they were some kind of revelation or something. You may get in a jam, especially since the names are not capitalized and often leap the spaces between the words. This makes it a real job to find them, but it'll provide a most fascinating few minutes for you. Yes, there are some really easy ones to spot, but don't get the big head cause truthfully you'll soon figure that it would take most federal judges and preachers numbers of hours to find them all. I admit that it usually takes a minister to find one of them and that is not uncommon for there are to be loud lamentations when it is pointed out. One lady says that when she is confronted with puzzles like this she brews a cup of tea to help her concentrate better, but then this gal's a real pro! Verbs, nouns, and all that stuff are her thing. See how well you can compete. Relax!! There really are twenty names of the Bible books in this story. If you fail to find them there's a penalty. You'll have to go fly a kite, sit on a banana, hum the battle hymn of the republic, or hose a dog (a mean one). Get to it!!

Heart to Heart: Devotional Thoughts for Women

Mystery Math

Take the number of years Methusaleh lived _____

Divide by the number of days Jonah was inside the great fish _____

Add the number of days of creation (including the day of rest) _____

Subtract the age of Jesus when He began His ministry
_____

Divide by the number of chapters in Genesis _____

Multiply by the number of people who passed by the injured man before the good Samaritan helped him
_____

Add the number of brothers the prodigal son had _____

Subtract the number of lepers Jesus healed (when only one returned to thank Him) _____

What is your final answer? _____

Rhyme Time

The following pairs of people had names that rhymed with each other. Can you name them?

1. Woman who hid spies in Jericho; King who opposed Elijah _____

2. Israelite king; Christian apostle _____

3. Prophet who fathered Maher-Shalal-Hash-Baz; Prophet who fathered Lo-Ruhamah and Lo-Ammi

4. Leader of Persian empire who released the Jews from captivity; Jewish official whose son was raised from the dead by Jesus _____

5. King who had 15 years added to his life; Prophet who bemoaned the fall of Jerusalem _____

6. Son of Abraham; Jacob's new name _____

Heart to Heart: Devotional Thoughts for Women

Can You Find The Common Link Between Each Set Of Items?

1. a sea, seasoning for speech, Lot's wife _____
2. Boaz, Obed, Jesse _____
3. merry, deceitful, hardened _____
4. lost donkeys, a tall man, anointing oil _____
5. shepherd, younger brother, murder victim _____
6. wedding surprise, stolen blessing, ladder to heaven _____
7. the prodigal son, Legion, casting pearls _____
8. Mahlon, Elimelech, Naomi _____
9. Unleavened bread, Weeks, Tabernacles _____
10. a fire, unruly evil, a world of iniquity _____

135

Answer Key

Matching puzzle, p. 43

1. Acts – f.
2. Exodus – h.
3. Genesis – d.
4. Isaiah – b.
5. Joshua – g.
6. Matthew – e.
7. Proverbs – j.
8. Psalms – c.
9. Revelation – i.
10. Romans – a.

Can You Figure This Out? p. 131

The answer to this was the word "whale". Whales were created without arms and legs and being animal, had no souls. A soul, Jonah, was placed inside a whale, but then was removed after three days. A whale's death used to provide light to people by burning the oil from inside the whale's body.

In the KJV of the Bible the word "whale" is used in the following passages: Genesis 1:21, Ezekiel 32:2, and Matthew 12:40. This last reference in Matthew refers to Jonah being in the belly of a whale.

Can You Find 20 Books of the Bible in this paragraph? p. 132

Someone showed me this story and re**mark**ed that there are twenty books of the Bible hidden here. He challenged me to find them. Sure enough they're all here.. Still this thing's a lu**lu, ke**pt me loo**king s**o hard for the longest time. Someone of you will get bogged down with **facts**, others are hit by them like they were some kind of **revelation** or something. You may get in a **jam, es**pecially since the names are not capitalized and often leap the spaces between the words. This makes it a real **job** to find them, but it'll provide **a most** fascinating few minutes for you. Y**es, there** are some really easy ones to spot, but don't get the big head cause **truth**fully you'll soon figure that it would take most federal **judges** and ***preacher**s **numbers** of hours to find them all. I admit tha**t it us**ually takes a minister to find one of them and that is not uncommon for there are to be loud **lamentations** when it is pointed out. One lady says that when she is confronted with puzzles like this s**he brews** a cup of tea to help her concentrate better, but then this gal's a real **pro! Verbs**, nouns, and all that stuff are her thing. See how well you can com**pete. R**elax!! There really are twenty names of the Bible books in this story. If you fail to find them there's a penalty. You'll have to go fly a kite, sit on a bana**na, hum** the battle hymn of the republic, or **hose a** dog (a mean one). Get to it!!

* "The book of the preacher" is another name for Ecclesiastes. I know, I know, I hear you groaning, but to be fair, I didn't make this puzzle up!

Mystery Math, p. 133

Take the number of years Methusaleh lived - 969

Divide by the number of days Jonah was inside the great fish – 3 (323)

Add the number of days of creation (including the day of rest) – 7 (330)

Subtract the age of Jesus when He began His ministry - 30 (300)

Divide by the number of chapters in Genesis – 50 (6)

Multiply by the number of people who passed by the injured man before the good Samaritan helped him - 2 (12)

Add the number of brothers the prodigal son had – 1 (13)

Subtract the number of lepers Jesus healed (when only one returned to thank Him) – 10 (3)

What is your final answer? 3

Rhyme Time, p. 134

1. Woman who hid spies in Jericho; King who opposed Elijah - Rahab/Ahab
2. Israelite king; Christian apostle - Saul/Paul
3. Prophet who fathered Maher-Shalal-Hash-Baz; Prophet who fathered Lo-Ruhamah and Lo-Ammi - Isaiah/Hosea
4. Leader of Persian empire who released the Jews from captivity; Jewish official whose son was

raised from the dead by Jesus - Darius/Jairus

5. King who had 15 years added to his life; Prophet who bemoaned the fall of Jerusalem – Hezekiah/Jeremiah

6. Son of Abraham; Jacob's new name – Ishmael/Israel

Can You Find the Common Link Between Each Set of Items? p. 135

1. a sea, seasoning for speech, Lot's wife - salt
2. Boaz, Obed, Jesse – relatives of David
3. merry, deceitful, hardened - heart
4. lost donkeys, a tall man, anointing oil – Saul
5. shepherd, younger brother, murder victim – Abel
6. wedding surprise, stolen blessing, ladder to heaven - Jacob
7. the prodigal son, Legion, casting pearls - swine
8. Mahlon, Elimelech, Naomi – relatives of Ruth
9. Unleavened bread, Weeks, Tabernacles - Feasts
10. a fire, unruly evil, a world of iniquity – the tongue

About The Author

Heather Pryor was born in Ohio and now resides in St. Petersburg, Florida. She has been married to her best friend and one true love, Paul, since 1988 and they have three children: Nicholas, Hannah, and Matthew. She has homeschooled her children all of their lives and graduated all three.

Heather enjoys working with and mentoring children and young ladies, and teaching and encouraging women in the Lord. For seven years she directed a Keepers at Home club for girls aged 7-18. She now spends her time developing Bible curriculum and media products for homeschools, families and churches through the family business, Pryor Convictions Media.

In her spare time, Heather enjoys baking, reading, a good cup of tea, and spending time with her husband and kids.

Made in the USA
Columbia, SC
01 May 2025